Herbert Brönner
Berlin Promotion Law

Berlin Promotion Law

in its version of February 18, 1976

including a brief commentary by
Dr. Dr. Herbert Brönner, Berlin
Wirtschaftsprüfer und Steuerberater
(Certified Public Accountant and Tax Adviser)

2nd edition

1976

W DE G

Walter de Gruyter · Berlin · New York

CIP-Kurztitelaufnahme der Deutschen Bibliothek

Berlin promotion law: in its version of February 18, 1976/including a brief commentary by Herbert Brönner. – 2. ed. – Berlin, New York: de Gruyter, 1976.
Einheitssacht.: Berlinförderungsgesetz ‹engl.›.
ISBN 3-11-007037-5
NE: Brönner, Herbert [Bearb.]; EST

Library of Congress Cataloging in Publication Data

Germany (Federal Republic, 1949–). Laws, statutes, etc.
Berlin promotion law in its version of February 18, 1976, including a brief commentary.
Translation of Berlinförderungsgesetz. Text in English and German.
Includes index.
1. Sales tax–Berlin. 2. Income tax–Berlin–Law. I. Brönner, Herbert, 1930– II. Title.
Law 343'.43'052 76-40929
ISBN 3-11-007037-5

Printing: W. Hildebrand, Berlin 65. – Binding: Berliner Buchbinderei Wübben & Co., Berlin 42

P R E F A C E

The American Chamber of Commerce in Germany welcomes the publication of the full text of the Berlin Promotion Law as a useful service to all those interested in investing in Berlin. This law, carefully annotated by Dr. Brönner, is of great importance to Berlin, because it makes both German and foreign investment in the city highly attractive.

The normalization of conditions in Berlin is expected to improve the business climate of the city considerably. It will intensify and normalize the integration of the West Berlin economy into that of the Federal Republic of Germany. Thus Dr. Brönner's annotated translation of the Berlin Promotion Law appears at a most timely moment when in particular American business interests considering investment in Germany will want to take a close look at the particular tax and other advantages Berlin has to offer.

Milan F. Ondrus
President
of the
American Chamber of Commerce in Germany

(September 1972)

INTRODUCTION

This publication is not an official translation of the Berlin Promotion Law. It is the outcome of the author's personal initiative. The purpose of this review is to make the law understandable to those not acquainted with the German language. Now as before, the German text is the sole authentic one. Consequently, it is advisable to make important decisions and to take significant steps based on the application of this law, only after having reconciled these procedures with the original German text and with the extensive administration of justice pertaining thereto. For understandable reasons, the author can assume no responsibility, regardless of its nature, for this translation.

Nevertheless, this limitation can not impair the value of this elaboration as a source of information. On the contrary, it expresses clearly that Berlin, even though organically connected with the largest industrial center on the continent, represents a sort of tax oasis. As such it is not even held suspect by the Revenue Authorities, but it is even benevolently supported on a legal basis. These advantages, coupled with further preferences, especially financial ones, should be brought to the notice of all those who have the intension of investing in Germany. This intention is accordant with the author's desire.

Experience has shown that every entrepreneur making speculations in this respect will have the following considerations in the foreground of the inquiry:

a) Turnover tax preferences (§§ 1, 1a, 2)
b) Special depreciation privileges (§ 14)
c) Investment grants (§ 19)
d) Tariff privileges

In the interpretation of this special law, an abundance of questions will of course arise which can mostly be clarified by open talks with the competent Revenue Authorities, if they have not already been cleared up elsewhere. Experience has shown that the Revenue Authorities are very open-minded in regard to serious investment projects in Berlin. At this point, a timely warning against improper interpretation of the legal regulations should be expressed. The Tax Adjustment Law provides the Revenue Authorities with the legal instruments necessary to ignore (as an exception) in such cases the design according to civil law and to tax on the basis of the true economic state of affairs.

Apart from this, the Berlin Promotion Law opens up exceedingly favourable tax conditions for serious entrepreneurial intentions in Berlin - and thereby in the Federal Republic of Germany, and at the same time in the area of the Common Market. This should be taken into consideration and should be made use of as far as possible.

Berlin, September 1972

Herbert Brönner

The Berlin Promotion Law has met with various adjustments; many open questions have been answered by jurisdiction.

This new translation and enlarged annotation will provide business interests considering starting or expanding investment in the city with the up-to-date information on the present state of advantages in both trading and investing in Berlin.

Berlin, March 1976

Herbert Brönner

Table of Contents

S e c t i o n I

PRIVILEGES WITH REGARD TO TURNOVER TAX, AND TAXES ON INCOME AND PROFIT; AWARDING OF INVESTMENT GRANTS

Article I
T u r n o v e r T a x P r i v i l e g e s

§ 1 Berlin Entrepreneur's Claim for Reduction

(1) If a Berlin entrepreneur has delivered goods to a West German entrepreneur, he is entitled to reduce the turnover tax he owes by 4.5% of the consideration agreed upon for the said objects, provided they have been made in Berlin (West) and have entered the remaining part of the purview of this law from Berlin.

(2) If a Berlin entrepreneur has supplied labour plus material in the remaining part of the purview of this law to a West German entrepreneur and has used objects made in Berlin (West) as component parts in this work, he is entitled to reduce the turnover tax he owes by 4.5% of the consideration for these objects, provided they have been separately invoiced.

(3) If a Berlin entrepreneur has performed services for a West German entrepreneur in Berlin (West), he is entitled to reduce the turnover tax he owes by 4.5% of the consideration agreed upon for these services, provided that the objects processed or finished have entered the remaining part of the purview of this law from Berlin (West).

(4) If a Berlin entrepreneur has leased objects to a West German entrepreneur, he is entitled to reduce the turnover tax he owes by 4.5% of the consideration agreed upon for turning over the said objects, provided they have been made by the Berlin entrepreneur after December 31, 1961 in Berlin (West) and have been utilized in the remeining part of the purview of this law.

(5) If a Berlin entrepreneur has turned over films, sound negatives or mixed tracks of synchronized versions to a West German entrepreneur for utilization in the remaining part of the purview of this law, he is entitled to reduce the turnover tax he owes by 4.5% of the consideration agreed upon for turn-

ing over the items for utilization, provided he has made them in Berlin (West) after December 31, 1961. Utilization in accordance with sentence 1 is turning over the objects for use by cinemas and for broadcasting by radio stations.

(6) If a Berlin entrepreneur has carried out any of the following services for a West German entrepreneur, he is entitled to reduce the turnover tax he owes by 10% of the consideration agreed upon for these services:

1. technical and economic advice and planning for plants out of Berlin (West), including the preparing of construction-, calculation- and plant records, as well as the supervision of carrying out any of these, provided the entrepreneur has been engaged in this exclusively, or substantially, in Berlin (West);
2. the turning over of industrial procedures, experience, and data processing programmes, which have - exclusively, or for the essential part - been developed or obtained in Berlin (West);
3. data processing with machines installed in Berlin (West);
4. the turning over of self-made designs for fashion purposes, model sketches and fashion photographs in Berlin (West);
5. other services rendered by publicity agents or advertising agencies as well as similar public relations enterprises involved usually or solely in advertising or the publicity business, provided the entrepreneur has been engaged in this exclusively or substantially in Berlin (West);
6. the services connected directly with the activities of film and television studios in Berlin (West) for the manufacture of image and sound carriers, as far as they are intended for utilization in the remaining part of the purview of this law; this does not apply to film and television studios operated by legal entities (under Public Law), or in the form of corporations according to private law, whose shares belong exclusively to corporations under public law and whose proceeds flow to juridical persons only;
7. the turning over of pre-printing and reprinting rights, as well as performance-, broadcasting- and screen rights, even for reproduction in extracts of works published in Berlin (West) and produced in Berlin (West);

8. the exploitation and transfer of information and newspaper publications by press clipping offices.

(7) In the cases of subsection 1 to 4, the percentage rate of reduction increases from 4.5 to 5, provided the objects have been made by a Berlin entrepreneur whose creation of additional value in Berlin (West) in the last fiscal year but one has amounted to more than 50% of the economic turnover allotted to Berlin (West). The percentage of reduction increases to 6% if the amount of value produced in Berlin (West) in the last fiscal year but one amounts to more than 65% of the economic turnover allotted to Berlin (West). The increased reduction will be granted only upon special application. A calculation of the additional value created in Berlin (West) according to a model determined by the Federal Minister of Economics is to accompany the application.

(8) The prerequisites for reductions according to the above subsections 1 - 7 are to be demonstrated by voucher (§§ 8,9) and by the books (§ 10).

ON § 1

Comment I. The turnover tax system in the Federal Republic of Germany (including Berlin West).

Comment II. Substantive law requirements for production preferences.

Comment III. Scope of the privileges.

Comment IV. Reduction claims and creation of additional value in Berlin (West).

C o m m e n t I

Since January 1, 1968 the turnover tax in Germany (the Federal Republic, including Berlin (West)) is imposed in the form of the so-called value-added tax. As a rule, the rate of tax is 11% of the consideration agreed upon, or in some special cases, 5 1/2%. In the invoices, the tax is to be separately listed so that the net price is clearly discernible. Tax paid as import tax, or shown in invoices separately by other entrepreneurs may be deducted by entrepreneurs as preliminary tax from their tax liability. As the deduction of preliminary tax is permissible even in case of export deliveries, though export in itself is exempt from turnover tax, there is to that extent a complete release from turnover tax. Only sales between entrepreneurs are taxable. An entrepreneur is anyone who independently carries out a business or professional activity. In the case of an integration of legally independent persons (natural or legal), or partnerships, there is an absence of independence and the sales are to be charged to the chief entrepreneur (Subsidiary, § 2 Turnover Tax Law). The integration must exist in a financial, an organizational and an economic respect. The entrepreneur's tax debt to the Revenue Office (§ 16 subsection 2 Turnover Tax Law) results from the difference between his own turnover tax and the permissible preliminary tax deduction. The tax burden can be reduced further by the privileges existing under the Berlin Promotion Law.

C o m m e n t II

The deliveries or services favoured must always be made or performed by a West Berlin entrepreneur for a West German (not a foreign) entrepreneur (cf. § 5). The deliveries favoured (subsection 1), including the supply of labour plus material (subsection 2), must be made in Berlin (West). In the case of rendering services (subsection 3), as well as in the performance of other services (subsection 6), they must be brought to completion exclusively, or at least substantially in Berlin (West) (cf. the Communication by the Federal Minister of Finances of November 12, 1970 - IV A/2 - S 7480 - 16/70 Federal Law Gazette 1970 I p. 1037). The objects leased (subsection 4) must have been made in Berlin (West) after December 31, 1961 and must be utilized in West Germany; the same applies to films, sound negatives and mixed tracks of synchronized versions (subsection 6). The privileges according to subsection 4 to 6 are granted only to producers not, as is the case in subsection 1, to dealers.

C o m m e n t III

(1) D e l i v e r i e s: The objects of the deliveries must have been made in Berlin (West) according to § 6 subsection 1. From January 1, 1976 the creation of additional value in this case has to amount to 10% (§ 6 subsection 2, in association

with § 31 subsection 2 number 2). The supplier is not required to have manufactured the objects himself, they may have been produced by another West Berlin entrepreneur. Deliveries of labour plus material made by a West Berlin entrepreneur to a West German entrepreneur are equated with deliveries (§ 1 subsection 2).

(2) Deliveries of Labour plus Material in the Area of Federal Republic: If objects in connection with this are made by a Berlin entrepreneur in Berlin (West), he is entitled to a turnover tax reduction, provided the objects are separately listed and charged in the invoice (Federal Ministry of Finances of April 1, 1958 Turnover Tax Law 1958, 85). Assembly costs in this connection do not enjoy these benefits (George, Berlin Tax Preferences, 5th edition, 1975, p. 20/21).

(3) Performance of Service Deliveries: This concerns the processing or finishing of a material provided by a West German party by a Berlin entrepreneur in Berlin (§ 1 subsection 3).

(4) Leasing: The turnover of a West Berlin entrepreneur is favoured, provided the objects were produced by him in Berlin (West) after December 31, 1961 and are thereafter utilized by a West German entrepreneur in West Germany. In case an object in Berlin (West) has to be assembled subsequently in West Germany e.g., telephone and data-processing installations, this is not detrimental to tax benefits.

(5) Films, Sound Negatives and Mixed Tracks of Synchronized Versions: Objects of this kind produced by a West Berlin entrepreneur and given to a West German entrepreneur for utilization - in a wide sense - makes his turnover favoured (§ 1 subsection 5).

(6) Various Other Services Rendered: In addition to deliveries and such-like, various other services, whose promotion is of special interest to Berlin, are listed at length in a catalogue. In the case of technical and economic advice in regard to installations out of Berlin (West) (e.g. factories, power plants, bridges and buildings) as well as in the turning over of industrial techniques, know-

how etc. (patents or other proprietary rights are not a prerequisite), it is decisive that the principal activity was carried out in Berlin (West), or that the technique was at least substantially developed or accomplished in Berlin (West). Data-processing favoured in accordance with this law is the utilization of units of data-processing installations, especially electronic ones, that subsequently convey the results to the party giving the order. The turning over of design for advertising purposes, (the forming of advertising ideas into words, sounds and pictures of model sketches, designs and patterns for the shaping of trade and industrial products) and fashion photos (pictures from the fashion sphere) is favoured provided the objects have been produced in Berlin (West) by the entrepreneur himself as can be demonstrated. Film and television studio services favoured are especially the production of films, magnetic tapes, magnetic plates and records by making use of the typical studio facilities provided that they are intended for utilization in West Germany. And finally the turning over of pre-printing and copying rights are favoured i.e. the turning over of a partial use of the publishing rights to the recipient of the services (e.g. publishers of periodicals), as a rule in the form of a licence contract in accordance with copyright. For further details in this regard, refer to the Communication of the Federal Minister of Finances of November 12, 1970 - IV A/2 - p 7480 - 16/70 (Federal Tax Gazette 1970 I, 1037) and, in particular, the Order of the Federal Minister of Finances of June 23, 1970 I, p 788).

Comment IV

The amount of the reduction claim in the cases under § 1 subsection 1 to 5 is 4.5%, in the cases of § 1 subsection 6 it is 10% of the consideration agreed upon (§ 7). In the cases under § 1 subsection 1 to 4 the reduction claim increases to 5%, provided the additional value created in Berlin (West) is more than 50% of the economic turnover allotted to Berlin (West), and to 6%, provided the additional value created in Berlin (West) is more than 65% of the economic turnover allotted to Berlin (West) (§ 1 subsection 7). The increased reduction is granted only if application is made on special forms. The term "additional value created in Berlin (West)" is explained in § 6 a. The basis of assessment with regard to certain objects e.g. meat, raw substances, kernel preparations, raw brandy and cigarettes, was expressly reduced by legislation (cf. § 4 subsection 2 to 6). Other objects were completely excluded from the benefit (§ 4 subsection 1). On sales effected after December 31, 1975 a creation of additional value of at least 10% is a condition to be entitled to the benefit (§ 6 subsection 2 in association with § 31 subsection 2). Legislation arranged the last year as the basis for the creation of additional value in order to enable the entrepreneur to make a timely calculation at the beginning of the year. Entrepreneurs who begin production in Berlin (West) for the first time may claim a reduction of 4.5% only. Increased reduction amounts may be claimed later, if the entrepreneur proves by a special calculation at the end of the first fiscal year that his creation of additional value during this first fiscal year was more than 50%, or more than 65% (Order of the Senator for Finances of November 19, 1970 Tax and Customs Gazette, Berlin, 1970, 1610, A II (4)).

§ 1 a Reduction Claims with Regard to Intrafirm Turnover

(1) If an entrepreneur has transferred objects he has made in a permanent business establishment in Berlin (West) to a West German permanent business establishment for industrial use, and if no claim exists according to § 1, the entrepreneur is entitled to reduce the turnover tax he owes by 6% of the amount charged (§7 subsection 3) for the objects transferred. The delivery of objects to purchasers in the remaining part of the purview of this law who are not West German entrepreneurs according to § 5 subsection 2 is not considered as industrial use, unless the objects have been processed or finished in the West German business establishment. The regulation of § 6 subsection 1 applies accordingly.

(2) The requirements for the reduction according to subsection 1 are to be demonstrated by vouchers and by the books.

ON § 1 a

Comment I. General Explanations
Comment II. Claim for Reduction

C o m m e n t I

In order to offer the West German economy an incentive to establish new places of business in Berlin (West), or to extend such places already in existence, the intrafirm turnover between the Berlin business establishment and the West German one belonging to the same enterprise have been benefited since January 1, 1970. This regulation applies also to enterprises having an interlocking relationship or those combined enterprises which form an entrepreneurial unit, but are independent enterprises as legal or natural persons according to the Civil Code. An intrafirm transaction in accordance with this regulation occurs when finished or unfinished goods produced in a business establishment in Berlin (West) have been transferred to a West German business establishment for industrial purpose and no reduction claim according to § 1 exists. According to the aims of this law only such procedures which, if the entrepreneur carried them out for third parties would be considered as deliveries, are to be favoured. In regard to the proof, compare with §§ 8, 9 and 10 of this law. According to this law, industrial use occurs if the object concerned is further processed, finished or utilized as part of the capital assets, used or consumed or delivered to a foreign buyer, or is used abroad in connection with a contract for delivery of labour and material. (Cf. Communication of Federal Minister of Finances of November 12, 1970 - IV A/2 p 7480 - 16/70, Federal Law Gazette 1970 I, 1037). A further requirement is that the object is materially transferred to the West German business establishment.

C o m m e n t II

The reduction claim amounts to 6% of the consideration appearing in the invoice, irrespective of the additional value created in Berlin. This is measured according to the regulations of § 7 subsection 3. The assessment basis of some articles e.g. meat, raw substances in bulk, kernel preparations, potable spirits was expressly reduced by legislation (cf. § 4 subsection 3). Other objects were completely excluded from the reduction claim (§ 4 subsection 1). In order to receive the benefit on intrafirm turnover, an additional creation of value of at least 10% is required on sales effected after December 31, 1975 (§ 6 subsection 2, in association with § 31 subsection 2). The Communications of the Federal Minister for Economics and Finances of December 14, 1971 - F/IV A 2 - p 7480 - 1871, German Tax Journal, Express Services of January 22, 1972 p. 25, express views as to what assessment basis is to be used in the calculation of the reduction according to § 1 a, if the objects subsequently enter the intrafirm traffic. As a matter of principle the domestic market price is therefore determinative in case of subsequent exporting. Should it be difficult to determine the domestic market price, then the entrepreneur may in individual cases use as a basis the actual export proceeds, insofar as they are obviously lower.

§ 2 Reduction Claims of West German Entrepreneurs

(1) If a West German entrepreneur has purchased objects from a Berlin entrepreneur, he is entitled to reduce the turnover tax he owes by 4.2% of the consideration invoiced for the objects, provided they have been made in Berlin (West) and have entered the remaining part of the purview of this law from Berlin (West).

(2) If a Berlin entrepreneur has used objects made in Berlin (West) as component parts in a contract delivery for labour plus materials to the remaining part of the purview of this law, the West German party placing the order is entitled to reduce the turnover tax he owes by 4.2% of the consideration for these objects, provided they have been separately invoiced.

(3) If a West German entrepreneur has had service deliveries performed by an entrepreneur in Berlin (West), he is entitled to reduce the turnover tax he owes by 4.2% of the consideration invoiced for these services, provided the processed and finished objects have entered the remaining part of the purview of this law from Berlin (West).

(4) If a West German entrepreneur has rented or leased objects from a Berlin entrepreneur, he is entitled to reduce the turnover tax he owes by 4.2% of the consideration entered into account for the objects turned over to him, provided they have been made by the Berlin entrepreneur after December 31, 1961 in West Berlin and have been utilized in the remaining part of the purview of this law.

(5) If a Berlin entrepreneur has turned over films, sound negatives or mixed tracks of synchronized versions to a West German entrepreneur for utilization in the remaining part of the purview of this law, the West German entrepreneur is entitled to reduce the turnover tax he owes by 4.2% of the consideration entered into account for the turning over of the objects for utilization by him, provided the said objects have been made by the Berlin entrepreneur in West Berlin after December 31, 1961. Utilization according to sentence 1 is the turning over of objects to cinemas, and to radio stations for broadcasting.

(6) If a Berlin entrepreneur has performed any other services designated in § 1 subsection 6 for a West German entrepreneur, the West German entrepreneur placing the order is entitled to reduce the turnover tax he owes by 4.2% of the consideration invoiced for these services.

(7) The prerequisites for reductions according to the above sections 1 - 6 are to be demonstrated by voucher (§§ 8, 9) and by book evidence (§ 10).

ON § 2

Comment I. General Explanations
Comment II. Reduction Claim

C o m m e n t I

The claim for reduction by Berlin entrepreneurs according to § 1 is complemented by the preferences according to § 2. According to the facts of the situation both regulations are congruent with each other. Even the requirements for the proof are of the same nature. There is therefore an implicit connection between the granting of the two preferences, i.e. if the requirements for the privileges to the Berlin entrepreneur are fulfilled, those for the West German entrepreneur are alsc met. Formal reasons can certainly give rise to differences. If one of the parties concerned fails to provide the evidence necessary (§§ 8, 9, 10) or if, for example, the evidence by voucher, or by the books, cannot be produced in a certain case.

C o m m e n t II

The reduction claim is a uniform 4.2% of the consideration invoiced, regardless of the additional value created, and quite independent of the fact whether the West German entrepreneur owes turnover tax or not. Thus the total amount of preference of the West German and of the Berlin entrepreneur taken together increases to at least 8.7.% and at the most to 10.2% of the consideration arranged.

§ 3 Restrictions on the Enterprise Sphere

Reductions according to §§ 1 and 2 will be granted only if the Berlin entrepreneur has carried out deliveries and performed other services within the scope of his own enterprise and for the business of the West German entrepreneur. § 5 subsection 2 No. 4 remains unaffected.

ON § 3

Comment I. General Explanations

C o m m e n t I

This is to ensure that transactions carried out in the private sphere, or even in the private sphere of one of the parties, do not benefit by §§ 1 and 2. For example, no privilege is granted on the delivery of consumer goods by a West Berlin entrepreneur to a West German private consumer.

§ 4 Exceptions, Restrictions

(1) The reductions according to § 1 subsection 1, § 1 a subsection 1 and § 2 subsection 1 will not be granted for the delivery, the transfer or the purchase of the following objects:

1. original works of plastic art, of painting and of the graphic arts of deceased artists;
2. used goods;
3. antiques;
4. postage stamps;
5. precious stones and jewelry (semi-precious stones), including synthetic ones, as well as any objects in combination

with such stones, except diamond tools (tools with a functioning part made of industrial diamonds);

6. genuine and synthetic pearls, as well as objects in combination with such pearls;
7. precious metals and alloys thereof in the form of raw and semi-finished materials as well as finished goods made of precious metals or their alloys (this does not include goods plated with precious metals or their alloys);
8. tin, bismuth, cadmium and alloys containing more than 20% tin or more than a total of 3% bismuth or cadmium, in the form of raw and semi-finished materials and of finished products, with the exception of pressure-casting products;
9. mercury;
10. such non-ferrous metals and their alloys not already listed under numbers 8 and 9 in the form of pre- and raw materials which have not been produced in Berlin (West) by a Berlin entrepreneur by means of thermal refining or alloying;
11. potable spirits according to the law on the Spirits Monopoly of April 8, 1922 (Reich Law Gazette I pp 335, 405) in the version in effect at the time, and semi-products for the production of potable spirits (except essences) which have been filled into containers of up to 10 litres in a West Berlin business establishment;
12. meat and edible slaughtering scraps from cows, calves, pigs and sheep, fresh, cooled or frozen; excepted are:
    a) meat and edible slaughtering scraps from animals butchered in Berlin (West) and cut up into the pieces usual in trade;
    b) meat obtained in Berlin (West) by complete deboning of heads, pigs-, calves- or sheep halves, as well as quarters of beef. Complete chop sections, pigs' heads, trotters and knuckles from pigs' halves, as well as heads, feet and tails of calves- and sheep halves need not be deboned. Deliveries and intrafirm turnover of these nondeboned objects are not favoured.
    c) meat from animal carcasses cut up in Berlin (West) and put into separate packages of up to 1000 grams;
13. a) roasted coffee (No. 09.01 A II of the Customs Tariff), unless all processing or finishing work necessary for the final product (except extraction of coffeine and

irritants), including standard sales packaging for final consumers (single packages up to 500 g), have been carried out in Berlin (West);

b) extracts and essences from coffee (No. 2101 A of the Customs Tariff) unless all processing and finishing work necessary for the final production of these articles (except the extraction of coffeine and irritants) have been carried out in Berlin (West);

14. cigarettes, tobacco and cigars unless all processing or finishing work necessary for the final production of these articles, including standard sales packaging for final consumers, have been carried out in Berlin (West);

15. scrap iron, junk- and waste material including waste by-products.

(2) In case a reduction is not already excluded by subsection 1, the reduction according to § 2 subsection 1 is not granted for the acquisition of the following goods:

1. raw substances (marzipan, peach-flavoured substitute for marzipan and nougat) and ke nel preparations (shelled or crushed almonds, hazelnuts, cashew nuts, apricot- and peach kernels);
2. potable spirits according to the Law on Spirits Monopoly of April 8, 1922 (Reich Law Gazette I pp 335, 405) in the version in effect atthe time, and for goods in process for the production of potable spirits, except essences racked into containers of up to 10 litres in a business establishment in Berlin (West);
3. meat and edible slaughtering scraps, if these items are listed in subsection 1 No. 12 letter a, letter b sentence 1 and letter c.

(3) In ase a reduction is not excluded by subsection 1 and 2, the consideration agreed upon or the internal transfer charge has to be reduced

1. for raw substances and kernel preparations (subsection 2 No. 1) as far as the reduction according to § 1 subsection 1 is concerned by 7%, as far as the reduction according to § 1 a subsection 1 is concerned by 50%;
2. for copper and its alloys in the form of pre- or raw material by 20%, provided the goods have been produced by a

Berlin entrepreneur, whose creation of additional value (§ 6 a) in the last year has amounted to at least 10% of his economic turnover allotted to Berlin (West), in other cases by 30%;

3. for potable spirits and goods in process for the production of potable spirits except essences (subsection 2 No. 2)
   a) as far as reductions according to § 1 subsection 1 are concerned by 14%, provided the goods have been produced by a Berlin entrepreneur, whose creation of additional value (§ 6 a) in the last year has amounted to at least 65% of his economic turnover allotted to Berlin (West), in other cases by 20%;
   b) as far as reductions according to § 1 a subsection 1 are concerned by 56%;
4. for meat and edible slaughtering scraps (subsection 2 No. 3) as far as reductions according to § 1 subsection 1 are concerned by 30%, as far as reductions according to § 1 a subsection 1 are concerned by 65%;
5. for roasted coffee (subsection 1 No. 13 letter a) as far as reductions according to § 1 subsection 1, § 1 a subsection 1 and § 2 subsection 1 are concerned by 60%;
6. for extracts and essences from coffee (subsection 1 No. 13 letter b) as far as reductions according to § 1 subsection 1, § 1 a subsection 1 and § 2 subsection 1 are concerned by 8.30 DM per kilogram, liquid objects by 8.30 DM per kilogram dried bulk, provided the calculation basis included the tax on coffee;
7. for cigarettes as far as reductions according to § 1 subsection 1 and § 1 a subsection 1 are concerned by 65%, as far as reductions according to § 2 subsection 1 are concerned by 58% provided the calculation basis includes the tax on tobacco;
8. for tobacco as far as reductions according to § 1 subsection 1, § 1 a subsection 1 and § 2 subsection 1 are concerned by 15% provided the calculation basis includes the tax on tobacco;
9. for other services benefiting public relations or advertising (§ 1 subsection 6 No. 5) as far as reductions according to § 1 subsection 6 and § 2 subsection 6 are concerned by the amount payable to third parties for performance of

the advertising operations.
The reductions of the consideration agreed upon or the internal transfer charge are to be proved by the books (§ 10). In the cases No. 6 and No. 9, the Berlin entrepreneur has to show the amount by which the consideration has to be reduced on the invoice and copies thereof.

(4) The Federal Government can determine by statutory order and with approval of the Bundesrat that the reduction according to § 1 subsection 1, § 1 a subsection 1, or § 2 subsection 1 will not apply, if, by these privileges, the existence of an important part of those West German entrepreneurs who supply objects of the same nature is considerably jeopardized.

ON § 4

Comment I. General Explanations
Comment II. Exceptions to the Claim for Reductions
Comment III. Restriction on the Claim for Reduction

C o m m e n t I

This regulation is a summary of all those exceptions and reductions of the preferences given on turnover tax which seem necessary with regard to economic considerations, no matter what their nature may be.

C o m m e n t II

The objects enumerated in subsection 1 are not given any preferences with regard to turnover under §§ 1, 1 a, and 2. In this connection, the term "used goods" is of special interest. This involves objects that are no longer new. In the jurisdiction of the courts up to now, reconditioned machines and similar objects have therefore been considered as used goods. The concession on objects for delivery consisting of used goods can therefore be granted only if a very small number of used parts (about 5% in relation to price) were used in the production thereof (Circular Disposition of the Superior Finance Directorate Berlin of October 28, 1966 Tax and Customs Gazette Berlin 1966, 1887). The regulation for an exception in § 4 subsection 1 No. 2 is also applicable in the following case:
A Berlin entrepreneur acquires a machine from an entrepreneur

in the Federal Republic and uses it in his enterprise. Some time later he sells the machine to another entrepreneur in West Germany. The privilege cannot be granted even if we assume that by using the machine in a Berlin enterprise, it became an object of different marketability (George, Berlin Tax Preferences, 5th edition. pp 58/59). With respect to the exceptions in the case of meat and edible slaughtering scraps, refer to the Communication of the Minister of Finances of November 12, 1970 - IV A/2 p 7480 - 16/70 (Federal Law Gazette 1970 I, 1037 under B V).

C o m m e n t III

According to the intention of the law to support labour and services performed in Berlin (West) you find a detailed list of more or less restricted preferences. The more single items have been produced or performed in Berlin (West), the higher the preference is, or - according to the system of the law - the lower is the reduction of the consideration agreed upon, which is the basis for the calculation of the normal (§ 1 subsection 1) reduction of turnover tax liability. Small quotas of labour or services within the consideration agreed upon lead to higher reduction rates of the price as the calculation basis (see in § 4 subsection 3 Nos. 4, 5, 7 and 9).

The reduction rates of the consideration agreed upon have been adjusted several times as the Berlin entrepreneur is quite flexible in working with this law and as - on the other hand - these rates must not lead to wrong and unintended economic results on the Berlin market.

§ 5 Berlin entrepreneurs, West German entrepreneurs

(1) According to this law, a Berlin entrepreneur is

1. an entrepreneur who has his management in Berlin (West) even with business establishments in the remaining part of the purview of this law, insofar as the regulation of subsection 2 No. 2 does not apply;
2. a business establishment located in Berlin (West) run by an entrepreneur whose management is situated in the remaining part of the purview of this law, or abroad.

(2) According to this law, a West German entrepreneur is

1. an entrepreneur who, with his business establishment in the remaining part of the purview of this law, has his management in the remaining part of the purview of this law;
2. a West Berlin entrepreneur's business establishment located in the remaining part of the purview of this law, if it has concluded the transaction with another West Berlin entrepreneur in its own name;
3. an entrepreneur's business establishment located in the remaining part of the purview of this law, whose management is situated outside of the remaining part of the purview of this law;
4. a corporation under public law and a political party in the remairing part of the purview of this law, even if deliveries and other services have not been carried out for their enterprise.

ON § 5

Comment I. General Explanation
Comment II. Berlin Entrepreneurs
Comment III. West German Entrepreneurs

Comment I

The term "enterprise" (as well as the term "entrepreneur") in accordance with this law conforms in essence with § 2 subsection 1 of the Turnover Tax Law. The two terms are however not identical, especially in light of the legal reappraisal of the concept "permanent business establishment" as used in this law. The concept of the "entrepreneur" goes beyond that of the persons engaged in a gainful activity, it includes also professional activities etc. The arranging of entrepreneurs according to area is of significance. The terms "Geschäftsleitung" (management of a firm) and "Betriebsstätte" (permanent business establishment) are defined in §§ 15 and 16 of the Tax Adjustment Law. According to § 15 of the Tax Adjustment Law, the center of the principal business management i.e. the place where decisive resolutions come into being, is the management of the firm. The legal location of the enterprise as a criterion to place the entrepreneur according to region is of no importance. According to § 16 of the Tax Adjustment Law a "Betriebsstätte" (business establishment) is any permanent local plant or establishment which serves for the pursuit of activities of a permanent business, among others the site of management, subsidiaries, manufacturing plants as well as other business facilities serving the entrepreneur or his permanent representative in the carrying on of the business. For the purpose of §§ 1 and 2, this term has been extended to include those persons engaged in the professional activities and entrepreneurs engaged in agriculture and forestry, while for § 1a only the limiting term of § 16 of the Tax Adjustment Law is applicable. (Wagner in "Neue Wirtschaftsbriefe" (NWB) Berlin, Division 17 Berlin p 122). To be taken into consideration is the fact that an entrepreneurial entity (with all the consequences to taxation) in accordance with this law is subordinated not only in the case of an entity according to civil law, but also in the case of the interlocking relationship between two companies in relation to turnover tax law, as well as the entrepreneurial entity, between the main office and the branch office in relation to turnover tax law. The subordination does not require a formal profit absorption agreement. The presence of this requirement according to German tax law is ascertained officially, purely on the basis of the actual facts of the case. These factors should therefore be taken into consideration in due time by the taxpayer. In the case of the existence of an interlocking entity or an entrepreneurial one, only intrafirm turnover is entitled to the application of § 1 a.

Comment II

A Berlin entrepreneur in accordance with subsection 1 of this law includes also a West German business establishment which delivers objects to other West German business establishments, insofar as these objects have been produced by an entrepreneur having his management in West Berlin to whose enterprise the supplying West German business establishment belongs. In addition, a Berlin entrepreneur is a business establishment located in Berlin belonging to an entrepreneur whose management is situated in West Germany or abroad. "It is not required that the Berlin business establishment act independently and in its own name. It can therefore market its products through a West German business establishment (the principal office, a branch office, parent or subsidiary company); that means the West German business establishment is permitted to accept the order, to deliver the goods and make out the invoice in its own name and collect the amount of the invoice." (See Sönksen-Hinnekens, Berlin Promotion Law - Berlin Finance Court - 1970, § 5 Explanation 5).

C o m m e n t III

West German entrepreneurs in accordance with this law include also those business establishments of entrepreneurs having their management in Berlin or abroad. The requirement for the granting of the benefit to West German business establishments belonging to a Berlin entrepreneur - this does not apply to entrepreneurs abroad - is that the transactions must be concluded with another Berlin entrepreneur in the firm's own name - among other things, on its own letterhead.

§ 6 Production in Berlin (West)

(1) Production in Berlin (West) occurs when by a processing or finishing operation in Berlin (West), according to the prevailing legal conception, an object of different marketability has come into being, unless the object has been only slightly worked. Marking, repacking, refilling, sorting, the making up of purchased goods into aggregates, and affixing of tax stamps are not considered as processing or finishing.

(2) A further requirement for production in Berlin (West) is that an object has been processed or finished by a West Berlin entrepreneur whose creation of additional value in Berlin (West) (§ 6 a) in the last fiscal year has amounted to at least 10% of the economic turnover allotted to Berlin (West).

This sentence 1 does not apply to objects listed in § 4 subsentence 2 No. 3 and subsentence 3 No. 2.

(3) Subsection 2 applies accordingly to performance of services. A performance of services by a West Berlin entrepreneur occurs also when he has the work carried out, completely or partially, by another West Berlin entrepreneur.

(4) Films are considered as having been produced in Berlin (West) if the studio-shooting has been carried out exclusively in West

Berlin studios and the technical services (cutting, musical recording, mixing and mass copy) have been carried out exclusively in Berlin (West). Sound negatives, and mixed tracks of synchronized versions are considered as having been produced in Berlin (West) if the technical services have been performed exclusively in Berlin (West).

ON § 6

Comment I. General Explanations
Comment II. Minimum Creation of Value

C o m m e n t I

The production must take place in Berlin (West); an activity changing the marketability by processing or finishing must occur; the process of production according to the given order must be finished in Berlin (West).
In order to obviate abuse, § 6 subsection 1 sentence 1 determines that the object may undergo not only slight processing in Berlin. There are no binding rules of interpretation in regard to this point. In cases of doubt, the competent tax authority of the "Land" (one of the main administrative districts of Germany e.g. Lower Saxony, Bavaria etc.) in agreement with the Senator for Economics in Berlin, who is the competent authority for the issue of the Certificate of Origin, will make the decision. The whole process of production inBerlin (West), and not the activity of any individual entrepreneur, is decisive.

C o m m e n t II

With regard to sales and intrafirm turnover carried out after December 31, 1975 the regulation of § 6 subsection 2 includes a further requirement for the granting of the benefit, the so-called average minimum creation of additional value. The creation of additional value by the Berlin entrepreneur processing or finishing the objects is decisive. While the "slightly worked object" applies to objects delivered etc., the minimum quota for the creation of additional value refers to the activity of the Berlin producer. The creation-of-additional-value quota is ascertained for the whole Berlin enterprise or for all parts of the Berlin enterprise (in case of enterprises with business establishments also outside of Berlin). If the conditions with regard to the Berlin producer in question are fulfilled, a dealer who buys from him and delivers to West Germany may possibly have to claim for reduction without detriment to his own creation-of-additional-value quota (George, Berlin Tax Preferences, 5th edition, p. 75). As the creation of additional value of the last fiscal year is used as a basis, the minimum production of additional value of 10% has to be achieved for the first time in the calendar year of 1974, or in the fiscal year ending in the calendar year of 1974.

§ 6 a Creation of Additional Value in Berlin

(1) According to section 1 subsection 7, and section 6 subsection 2, the creation of additional value in Berlin is the difference between the economic turnover and the economic input of material by the Berlin entrepreneur's business establishment located in Berlin (West). The economic turnover is considered to be the work done by the Berlin entrepreneur in the production of objects and in the performance of services in Berlin (West) on the basis of sales prices without turnover tax. The economic input of material attributed to the economic turnover is considered as the consumption of raw materials, auxiliary materials and operating supplies, including the performance of services made use of, on the basis of the acquisition cost. Taxes on tobacco, spirits and coffee are not entered into account to ascertain the Berlin creation of additional value, insofar as the Berlin entrepreneur has paid such taxes.

(2) In the ascertainment of the economic input of materials, allowances can be made for preliminary performance in Berlin as follows:

1. If the economic use of materials contains objects which another entrepreneur has produced in Berlin (West), as can be demonstrated, 60% of the declared value of these objects can be eliminated from the economic input of materials. This sentence 1 does not apply to objects, for the delivery, transfer or purchase of which according to § 4 subsentence 1 a reduction is not granted.
2. If the economic input of materials contains services performed by another entrepreneur in Berlin (West), as can be

demonstrated, the value assessed for these services can be eliminated from the economic input of materials.

(3) By statutory order, the Federal Government, with the approval of the Bundesrat, can more closely determine the extent of the economic turnover and economic input of material in order to maintain uniformity of taxation, remove inequality in cases of hardship, or simplify taxation procedures.

ON § 6 a

Comment	I.	General Explanations
Comment	II.	Economic Turnover and Economic Materials Input
Comment	III.	Value of the Berlin Performance of Work with Regard to Taxation

Comment I

The regulation concerning the creation of additional value is the principal point in the amendment to the Berlin Aid Law of June 23, 1970. The purpose of it is to provide an additional inducement to intensify production in Berlin and thereby make a contribution towards strengthening the economy in Berlin. According to § 1 subsection 7, a higher reduction rate in the turnover tax is granted on application in the case of a high creation of additional value in Berlin. The law takes the average creation of additional value in the production sphere of the processing or finishing by the Berlin producer in all his Berlin business establishments as a criterion.
Legally independent enterprises combined by an interlocking arrangement or by entrepreneurial unity are here considered as business establishments belonging to the same enterprise.
According to § 10 subsection 1, the requirements with regard to book evidence, especially the amount of the Berlin creation of value, must be clear and easy to check from the accounts and other records. With regard to details concerning this problem, refer also to the Order of the Senator for Finances of November 19, 1970 (Tax and Customs Gazette 1970, 1610).

Comment II

The economic turnover is composed of the following parts:
1. proceeds from deliveries of manufactured objects (i.e. ex-

cluding commercial articles) and from the supply of labour and materials to third parties,

2. changes in the inventories of the finished and unfinished products,
3. so-called intrafirm services (fictitious deliveries and fictitious supplies of labour and materials to part of the enterprise outside of Berlin),
4. other services within the internal sphere entered as assets.

The proceeds from sales are to be shown in the accounts without turnover tax but after deduction of decreases (bonuses, discounts, rebates). Deviating from the balance sheet, changes in the inventories are to be valued on the basis of the sales prices. Internal performances occur also, for example, when products manufactured in Berlin are utilized as part of the capital assets in foreign business establishments (for details refer to the Order of the Senator for Finances of November 19, 1970 cited under Comment I).

The economic materials input is considered to be the consumption of raw and auxiliary materials and operating supplies, including services performed which were made use of, calculated on the basis of costs, relative to the economic turnover. However, only the consumption of such materials which can be attributed to the sphere of production and to the performance of services are to be taken into account. Taxes on tobacco and spirits are not taken into consideration in the ascertainment of the Berlin creation of value, insofar as the Berlin entrepreneur himself has paid these taxes. The Tax Authorities have worked out a special form for the calculation of the Berlin creation of value, which is to be taken as a basis at all times.

Comment III

Services performed in Berlin relevant to taxation can be taken into account with regard to the ascertainment of the Berlin creation of value. The value of objects produced in Berlin can be eliminated from the materials input to the amount of 60%. The value of services performed in Berlin can be eliminated to the full extent. The Order of the Senator for Finances of November 19, 1970 (see Comment I) provides a regulation for this.

§ 7 Basis of Assessment

(1) According to this law, the turnover tax does not pertain to consideration. § 10 subsection 1 of the Turnover Tax Law (value-added tax) is to be applied. If the Berlin entrepreneur pays tax on his turnover according to § 19 subsection 1 of the Turnover Tax Law (value-added tax), reductions according to the §§ 1 and 2 are to be made in the consideration including the turnover tax. The same applies to reductions according to § 13.

(2) In §§ 1 and 13 the considerations received take the place of the considerations agreed upon, if the entrepreneur calculates the turnover taxes according to considerations received (§§ 19 and 20 of the Turnover Tax Law (value-added tax)). In such cases the equivalent received and the day of receipt, instead of the considerations agreed upon, is to be proved by book evidence. In case of a change in the manner of taxation, reduction amounts may not be claimed twice.

(3) The internal transfer price according to § 1 a subsection 1 is represented by the amount the entrepreneur would have had to pay to a foreign entrepreneur to obtain the object that was transferred to a West German business establishment (market price less turnover tax). If an internal transfer price cannot be ascertained in this manner, the reduction is to be based on 115%, at the most, of the production costs as calculated according to income tax regulations.

ON § 7

Comment I. Consideration
Comment II. Internal Transfer Price

C o m m e n t I

Consideration consists of every thing that the West German entrepreneur has to spend according to agreement, including the incidental expenses such as packing charges, forwarding charges, etc. insofar as the customer has to bear them. Basically, the consideration arranged is decisive. If the Berlin entrepreneur, however, pays taxes according to the consideration received, which is permissible, this will be the basis of assessment.

C o m m e n t II

With regard to intrafirm turnover the so-called internal transfer price takes the place of consideration. Here a sort of fictitious purchase price in the form of the market price (without turnover tax) or better in the form of a reseller's purchase price is used as a basis. This also applies even if the product transferred to the West German business establishment is subsequently exported. If the object is subsequently invested in a foreign business establishment as part of the fixed assets, the same applies. Even if the prices on the foreign markets are lower, the higher price on domestic markets remains the calculation basis. (Turnover Tax Law View 1972, p. 32).

If a market price cannot be determined, for example because the object is not marketed in this form, the reduction is to be based on no more than 115% of the production costs calculated according to the regulations of the Income Tax Law. As this lump sum maximum value serves the purpose of simplification and of prevention of abuse, any other form of valuation (e.g. at cost) is not permissible (Communication of the Federal Minister of Finances of November 12, 1970 - IV A/2 - p 7480 - 16/70, Federal Tax Gazette 1970 I, 1037).

§ 8 Certificate of Origin

(1) Evidence that an object has been made or that a service has been performed in Berlin (West) is to be demonstrated by a Certificate of Origin, which the Senator for Economics in Berlin will issue on application by the Berlin entrepreneur. The application is to be made by presenting invoices or delivery notes, and by providing assurance that the prerequisites of manufacture in Berlin (West) (§ 6) have been fulfilled. As a matter of principle, the Certificate of Origin will be issued in duplicate, one copy of which is intended for the West German entrepreneur. On application the Senator for Economics, Berlin, may give permission to Berlin entrepreneurs to issue the Certificate of Origin themselves.

(2) Section 1 applies by the same token to other services according to § 1 subsection 6 and section 2 subsection 6.

(3) The Senator for Economics, Berlin, determines the details of procedure. He is authorized to demand from the entrepreneur statements and supporting documents to ascertain the facts of the case, as well as about the extent of Berlin creation of value. The Revenue Offices can supply the information required.

(4) In public law disputes concerning the issue of the Certificate of Origin, the stages of appeal for financial affairs are the competent ones.

ON § 8

Comment I. General Explanations

C o m m e n t I

The requirement in order to obtain the turnover tax benefits is proof in the form of the Certificate of Origin. This document is issued by the Senator for Economics, Berlin (Martin-Luther-Straße 105, 1000 Berlin 62), if the entrepreneur has not already been given permission to issue the Certificate of Origin himself (simplification of the administrative procedure). In case of necessity, the details of procedure can be obtained from the Senator for Economics on inquiry.

§ 9 Evidence of Shipping and Conveyance

(1) In the purview of this law, evidence by a shipping voucher, especially by a consignment note, certificate of posting, original bill of lading, or duplicate thereof, or by any other voucher customary in the trade, especially by a certification from the forwarding agent commissioned by the entrepreneur, or by a certification of receipt from the business establishment, or from the purchaser, or from the customer in the remaining part of the purview of this law, is to be demonstrated that the objects designated in § 1 subsection 1 to 3, § 1 a subsection 1 and § 2 subsection 1 to 3 have entered the remaining part of the purview of this law. The kind of voucher described above as "any other" has to disclose at least the usual trade designation of the objects, the day of shipping or conveyance and the means of conveyance (e.g. railway, or motor truck). Furthermore, the voucher is to contain the issuer's assurance that the information given in the voucher was made on the basis

of business records, which can be verified in the purview of this law.

(2) Evidence that the objects designated in § 1 subsection 4 and 5 will be used or utilized in the remaining part of the purview of this law is to be furnished by a certificate from the West German entrepreneur indicating the period of time for their use or utilization.

(3) In well-founded cases the Revenue Office may on application permit evidence to be demonstrated by means of other business records.

ON § 9

Comment I. General Explanations

C o m m e n t I

This proof is also to be adduced in any case. The Berlin Tax Authority has permitted simplification in some cases. With regard to details concerning this matter, refer to George, Berlin Tax Preferences, 5th edition, pp. 104-106.

§ 10 Book Evidence

(1) The conditions to be satisfied by book evidence must be clear and easy to verify from the accounts. The accounts are to be kept in the purview of this law.

(2) As a rule, the following items are to be recorded

1. for reductions according to § 1:
   a) the quantity and the usual trade designation of the objects that have been delivered, processed or finished for remunderation,
   b) the production of the objects or the performance of service deliveries in Berlin (West) with reference to the certificate of origin (§ 8),
   c) the supplier and the date of delivery to the Berlin entrepreneur, or the party performing the service delivery and the date of the performance for the Berlin entrepreneur, if the Berlin entrepreneur has neither produced, nor processed nor finished the object himself,
   d) the nature of the services according to § 1 subsection 6

with reference to the certificate of origin (§ 8),

e) the recipient of the consignment or of the other services in the remaining part of the purview of this law by name, designation of the industry or occupation and address,

f) the date of shipping or transportation of the object delivered or finished with reference to the shipping records or other vouchers (§ 9 subsection 1),

g) the period of time during which the objects leased have been used in the purview of this law, or when the films, sound negatives or mixed tracks of synchronized versions have been utilized in the remaining part of the purview of this law with reference to the certificates pertaining thereto issued by the West German entrepreneur (§ 9 subsection 2),

h) in cases under § 1 subsection 7, the calculation of the Berlin creation of additional value,

i) in cases under § 6 a subsection 2, the nature of the Berlin preliminary production with reference to the invoice received and the certificate of origin (§ 8),

j) the consideration agreed upon with reference to a copy of the invoice,

k) the amount by which the consideration agreed upon has to be reduced in cases under § 4 subsection 3,

2. for reductions according to § 1 a:

a) the quantity and the usual trade designation of the objects transferred to a West German business establishment,

b) the production of the objects in a West Berlin business establishment with reference to the certificate of origin (§ 8),

c) the day on which the objects arrived at the West German business establishment,

d) the use of the objects,

e) the internal transfer price, and the manner of ascertaining it,

f) the amount by which the internal transfer charge is to be reduced in cases under § 4 subsection 3,

3. for reductions according to § 2:

a) the quantity and the usual trade designation of the objects purchased, or processed or finished for remundera-tion,

b) the supplying firm or the party performing the services,
c) the place of manufacture or the place of the performance of service with reference to the certificate of origin (§ 8),
d) the nature of the other services according to § 2 sub-section 6 with reference to the certificate of origin (§ 8),
e) the day of receipt of the objects in the remaining part of the purview of this law with reference to the bill of lading or vouchers,
f) the period of time during which the leased objects were used in the remaining part of the purview of this law, or when the film, sound negatives, or mixed tracks of synchronized versions were utilized in the remaining part of the purview of this law,
g) the consideration agreed upon with reference to the in-voice received,
h) the amount by which the consideration agreed upon has to be reduced in cases under § 4 subsection 3.

(3) the Revenue Office may permit a fiscally reliable entre-preneur to produce evidence recorded in a different manner.

ON § 10

Comment I. General Explanations

C o m m e n t I

The conditions for the tax benefits are that the evidence must be easy to demonstrate and verify according to the books within the country. The evidence by the books is a requirement of substantive law for the turnover tax reductions. Errors or deficiencies in the book evidence consequently preclude the reduction as a matter of principle. Slight deficiencies can in certain circumstances be remedied. The absence of required information does not oblige the Revenue Office to refuse the benefits, if the evidence is considered as furnished on the basis of the complete accounts. Beyond that, the Revenue Office may apriori allow such enterprises that are fiscally reliable easier methods of providing book evidence. (Sönksen-Hinnekens, Berlin Promotion Law - Berlin Finance Court - 1970, § 10 Explanation 5).

§ 11 Reduction Procedures

(1) The reduction amounts according to §§ 1, 1 a and 2 are to be set off against the turnover tax due for a preliminary declaration period or period of assessment. § 18 subsection 2 sentence 4 and 5, and subsection 4 sentence 4 of the Turnover Tax Law (value-added tax) are to be applied.

(2) In case that reductions are made in considerations, or internal transfer price, the amounts of reduction according to § 1, 1 a and 2 are to be refunded, insofar as they concern the reduced consideration. The amount to be refunded is to be added to the tax due for the preliminary declaration period (period of assessment) during which the considerations have been reduced.

(3) Subsection 2 applies accordingly when consideration agreed upon is not recoverable. Should the considerations be received subsequently, then the entrepreneur may make the reduction anew.

ON § 11

Comment I. General Explanations

C o m m e n t I

The entrepreneur who is privileged may reduce the turnover tax he owes by the amount of the reduction for the existing preliminary declaration period or the assessment period, that means normally monthly. If there is no turnover tax debt, or an insufficient one, the entrepreneur is entitled to claim a refund.

§ 12 Lapse of Reduction Claims

If objects, for whose transfer or purchase a reduction claim exists according to §§ 1 or 2, have been returned to Berlin (West) without having been subjected to processing or finishing in the remaining part of the purview of this law according to § 6 subsection 1, the reduction in the turnover tax due may not be made. If the West German entrepreneur returns the objects to the Berlin supplier, the reduction according to § 1 may not be made. If the reduction has already been made, the amount of reduction is to be refunded to the Revenue Office.

ON § 12

Comment I. General Explanations

C o m m e n t I

In cases of redelivery to Berlin, for whatever reason, all preferences will, as a rule, lapse.

§ 13 Special Reduction Claims for Entrepreneurs in Berlin (West)

(1) Entrepreneurs for whose turnover taxation a Revenue Office in Berlin (West) is competent (§ 73 subsection 4 of the Reich Impost Ordinance), and whose total turnover (§ 9 subsection 3 of the Turnover Tax Law (value-added tax) in the current calendar year does not exceed 200,000.-- Deutsche Mark, are entitled to reduce their turnover tax due for a preliminary declaration period (assessment period) by 4% of the consideration for the taxable sales effected within the same period of time without detriment to their reductions according to § 1, 1 a, and 2. The amount of reduction may not exceed 720 Deutsche Mark for the calendar year. If the total turnover consists exclusively of returns from professional activities according to § 18 subsection 1 No. 1 of the Income Tax Law, or from work as a commercial representative or broker, the maximum amount of reduction in a calendar year is 1200 Deutsche Mark. § 18 subsection 2 sentences 4 and 5, and subsection 4 sentence 4 of the Turnover Tax Law (value-added tax) is to be applied.

(2) If the total turnover includes returns from professional activity or work as a commercial representative or broker, as well as of other receipts, a reduction of up to 1200 Deutsche Mark in respect to the first-mentioned returns may be made. If, in the case of these returns, an amount lower than 1200 Deutsche Mark results, the balance of the reduction amount, not exceeding 720 Deutsche Mark, may be deducted from turnover tax due on other receipts.

(3) Entrepreneurs, according to subsection 1, whose total turnover exceeds 200,000 Deutsche Mark in the current calendar year, may deduct from the turnover tax they owe an amount to be calculated as follows: The amount which would be deductible if the turnover limit of 200,000 Deutsche Mark were not taken into consideration is reduced by 4% of the amount by which the total turnover exceeds 200,000 Deutsche Mark.

ON § 13

Comment I. General Explanation

Comment I

This deals with special benefits for entrepreneurs who have a turnover in a calendar year of about or below 200,000 Deutsche Mark, such as members of the liberal professions (physicians, lawyers, certified public accountants, etc.), commercial representatives and brokers. These benefits depend on the development of turnover tax rights in Germany.

Article II

Income Tax Privileges

§ 13 a Special Regulations for the Application of § 6 a and § 7 Subsection 2 of the Income Tax Law

(1) Calculating the fractional value of a pension obligation the rate of interest amounts to at least 3.5% deviating from § 6 a subsection 3 last sentence of the Income Tax Law in case

1. the pension obligation was established before the end of employment of the pension holder provided he had been employed in a permanent business establishment in Berlin (West) for more than 8 months during this fiscal year;
2. the pension reserve was established after the end of employment under maintenance of the pension in reversion or in case of pension payment provided the pension holder had been employed in a permanent business establishment in Berlin (West) for more than 8 months during the last fiscal year prior to the end of employment or the case of pension payment.

(2) For movable assets which belong to the capital assets of a

permanent business establishment in Berlin (West) and remain-in it for more than 3 years after their acquisition or production, § 7 subsection 2 sentence 2 of the Income Tax Law 1958 (Federal Law Gazette I, p. 672) remains applicable.

ON § 13 a

Comment General Explanations

These regulations have given preference to Berlin according to § 53 subsection 1 and 2 of the Income Tax Law. They have been taken into the Berlin Promotion Law without any substantial change for systematic reasons only.

§ 14 Increased Depreciation Provisions for Depreciable Fixed Assets

(1) Instead of the depreciation rate applicable according to § 7 of the Income Tax Law allowances of up to 75% of the acquisition costs may be obtained within the fiscal year of acquisition or production and the following four fiscal years for asset items subject to wear and tear as designated in subsection 2, which are part of the fixed assets of a business establishment in Berlin (West). The depreciation of movable assets is to be rated in equal annual amounts according to the remaining net book value and the estimated useful life of the asset in question from the fiscal year on, when increased allowances may no longer be made at the latest from the fifth year after the fiscal year of acquisition or production onward; the depreciation of buildings is to be rated on the percentage according to § 7 subsection 4 of the Income Tax Law in consideration of the residual book value and the remaining anticipated useful life.

(2) Increased allowance according to subsection 1 can be claimed

1. with regard to movable assets remaining in a business establishment in Berlin (West) for at least three years after their acquisition or production
2. with regard to buildings which have been erected in Berlin (West) and
   a) which serve directly for more than 80% of the firm's own business in

aa) manufacturing of economic goods intended for sale or producing energy or heat or
bb) processing of economic goods intended for sale or
cc) restoration of economic goods or
dd) research or development according to § 51 subsection 1 No. 2, letter 4 sentence 4 of the Income Tax Law or
ee) the management or administration or storing of inventories in connection with the activities designated above in aa to dd or

b) which serve by more than 80% as dwellings for people in the firm's own employment.

Regarding ships, the regulation of sentence 1 No. 1 is applicable with a period of eight instead of three years; in case a ship is acquired, a further requirement for the application of sentence 1 is that the ship has been obtained in an unused condition from the manufacturer.

(3) Increased allowances according to subsection 1 can also be claimed for the development and extension of existing buildings, provided the developed or newly-made parts of the buildings fulfill the requirements of subsection 2 No. 2. The increased allowances in this case are rated according to the production costs disbursed for the development or expansion. From that year onwards when increased allowances according to sentence 1 may no longer be made, the residual value is to be added to the original costs or the construction costs of the building, or the value taking their place; further allowances for wear and tear to the building are to be rated uniformly for the whole building according to the amount resulting herefrom and to the percentage applicable for the building.

(4) According to subsection 1 and 3, increased provision for depreciation may already be made on prepayments for costs and on partial construction costs.

(5) § 7 a subsection 6 Income Tax Law is not applicable.

(6) The regulations of § 14 of the Berlin Aid Law in its version of August 19, 1964 (Federal Law Gazette I p. 674) remain applicable to buildings whose construction was begun before January 1, 1970 and was finished before January 1, 1975.

ON § 14

Comment I. General Explanations
Comment II. Persons Favoured
Comment III. Scope of Privileges

C o m m e n t I

The financing alleviation represented by every increased depreciation allowance is intended to be an inducement to greater investments in Berlin (West). The expenditure, or loss arising herefrom may be offset by other profits or carried over into later assessment periods. This provides the possibility of spreading losses over relatively long periods of time: According to § 14 Berlin Promotion Law, special depreciation amounts may be distributed at discretion over the year of acquisition or production, as well as over the following four fiscal years. According to § 10 of the Income Tax Law, the losses of the preceding five years incurred by persons carrying on an industry, craft or trade may be deducted for tax purposes. All in all, such specially allowed depreciation losses can therefore be set off against the current profits of ten fiscal years. The specially allowed depreciation amounts diminish the income or corporation income tax, as well as the trade tax on profits.

As a requirement for taking advantage of the benefit, the asset items must enter a current index, unless the date of acquisition or production, historic costs, usefull life of the asset and the annual rate of depreciation can easily be gained from the books.

The term "Betriebsstätte" is to be construed in accordance with § 16 of the Tax Adjustment Law. A "Betriebsstätte" may be defined as a permanent local establishment or plant which serves the purpose of making a profit (Masuch, Neue Wirtschafts-Briefe (NWB), Berlin, Subject 3 Berlin p. 564).

C o m m e n t II

All persons subject to taxation, regardless of their legal form, who meet the requirements mentioned may lay claim to the increased depreciation allowance. This applies to persons having a residence or their usual abode in Berlin, and to corporations with their registered office or management at home or abroad, insofar as they maintain a business establishment in Berlin (West) only. The Leasing Order of the Federal Minister of Finance of April 19, 1971 (Federal Tax Gazette I p. 264) regulates who can claim increased depreciation allowances on movable asset items in the case of leasing agreements. With regard to immovable assets (buildings), the Communication of March 21, 1972 (F/IV B 2/P 2170/11/72) regulates who can claim.

C o m m e n t III

The benefit covers costs of acquisition or production, and deposits on costs of acquisition as well as partial costs of production. Costs of acquisition include incidentals to the acquisition such as transport and assembly costs, however without turnover tax. With regard to buildings, costs of production may, under certain conditions, include the costs of demolition, but on the other hand not the expenditure for the acquisition of the bare structure of a building (Federal Finance Court of November 21, 1969, Feder Law Gazette 1970 II, 118).

It is to be emphasized that increased depreciation allowances may already be made on down payments in case of acquisition, and partial production costs in case of construction. If deposits are made by cheque or bill of change, payment is not effected until the bill of change is discounted or the cheque has been credited to account (§ 7 a subsection 2 Income Tax Law 1975).

The depreciation of material, not immaterial, asset items of the capital assets, insofar as they are depreciable, are favoured. With the exception of ships, the acquisition of such goods need not be a question of "unused", i.e. new objects.

The increased depreciation allowances of up to 75% may be made during the year of acquisition or production as well as in the following four fiscal years. The distribution over this period of time is optional, i.e. there is also a possibility of writing off the special depreciation of 75% already in the first year. In case of individual asset items, the procedure may also vary. With regard to the residual value, refer to the Order of the Senator for Finances of February 1, 1960 (Federal

Law Gazette, Berlin 1960, 75).

It is to be mentioned that the new and general regulation of § 7 a subsection 6 Income Tax Law 1975 according to which increased depreciation rates must not cause or increase losses expressly does not apply to cases under Berlin Promotion Law (§ 14 subsection 5). This is an added attraction to entrepreneurial activities in Berlin especially regarding § 10 d Income Tax Law, which allows losses to be carried forward for five years and set off against future profits.

A special factor to be observed with regard to movable asset items is evidence of the three-year time limit. It is sufficient if the asset item remains as part of the capital assets in a business establishment in Berlin for a period of three years. It may also be in a business establishment in Berlin belonging to another entrepreneur, e.g. in the case of sale, leasing, etc. With regard to vehicles, it is of importance that they must be used chiefly in Berlin traffic. The cancellation of the benefits on account of premature separation, as provided by legislation, lapses if the separation is based on an occurance "not lying within the sphere of the will" of the taxpayer (Administrational Court of Berlin of April 7, 1964, Decision of the Finance Court 1964, 523) e.g. Act of God, or a useful service life of less than three years etc.

In comparison with the past, the benefits with regard to buildings have been substantially reduced since 1970. Factory buildings as well as workshops for the handicrafts serve as place of manufacture. In respect of annexes, refer to the Order of the Senator for Finance of September 9, 1968 (Tax Gazette Berlin 1968, 1970). The term "building" depends on aspects related to taxation laws and is not identical with the word as used in Civil Law. In the meantime extensive court jurisdiction has evolved on fixing the limits of buildings on the one hand, and those of movable asset items on the other. Therefore, air houses for example, insofar as they have no solid contact with the ground, have as a rule been considered to be movable assets. (Finance Ministry, North Rhine Westphalia 1971, "Finanz Rundschau" 1971 p. 588). According to George (Berlin Tax Preferences, 5th edition, p. 162), the application of § 14 with regard to buildings depends solely on the actual conditions in the fiscal year or the calendar year in which the claim for increased depreciation is to be asserted. If, after taking advantage of the permissible privileges, the conditions of § 14 subsection 2 No. 2 no longer exist, the privileges will not be cancelled.

The special depreciation allowances offer an exeptional attraction for entrepreneurial associations in the legal form of personal associations. The Revenue Department has accepted the present arrangement that partners having recently joined the firm can share fully, until completion of the building, in the production costs and special depreciation allowances pertaining thereto. That means even if several years of building time are required and the partners join the firm, for example, only during the last year (the year of completion), they are entitled to full participation. As a matter of principle, adverse capital accounts of the co-entrepreneurs in personal association are acknowledged herein.

The possibility of taking advantage of special depreciation allowances in different rates by the individual partners has been limited to asset items acquired or produced before January 1, 1975.

The liquidation of the hidden reserve built up by the special depreciation allowance is effected by decreased writing off during the following years or by later sale of the asset before expiry of the period of use. To avoid the removal of economic strength from Berlin by the displacement of the hidden reserves, the three-year period was introduced in the case of movable assets. With regard to buildings, such a displacement is possible under § 6 b of the Income Tax Law. However, experience has shown that a transfer of ownership is difficult in respect of this, as a purchaser cannot repeat the special depreciation allowances on buildings, and this fact is taken into consideration in fixing the purchase price.

§ 14 a Increased Depreciation Allowances on Residential Premises and Condominium Apartments

(1) On buildings and condominium apartments built under the tax privilege program or the privately financed housing program in Berlin (West), and which have been used by more than

80% for at least three years for residential purposes, the party giving the building order can, notwithstanding § 7 subsection 4 and 5 of the Income Tax Law, make increased allowances of up to a total of 50% of the construction costs in the year of completion of the building and in the following two years. From that year on when increased allowances may not be made, at the latest starting from the third year after the completion of the building, the depreciation is to be treated according to the residual value and the decisive percentage applicable according to § 7 subsection 4 of the Income Tax Law, taking into consideration the remaining useful life. If the construction costs of a single-family house or a condominium apartment exceed 150,000 Deutsche Mark, or in the case of a two-family house 200,000 Deutsche Mark, the regulations of § 7 subsection 4 of the Income Tax Law are to be applied to the excessive amount of the construction costs.

(2) Increased allowances according to subsection 1 sentence 1 can also be claimed for the development and extension of buildings and cooperative apartments in Berlin (West), provided the developments or extensions were completed under the tax privilege or privately financed housing program and if the developed or newly constructed parts of the buildings were used by more than 80% for at least three years for residential purposes. The increased allowances in this case are rated according to the construction costs disbursed for the development or extension. Subsection 1 sentence 3 applies accordingly. From that year on when increased allowances may not be made, the residual value is to be added to the acquisition or construction costs of the building or condominium apartment or to the value taking their place; the further allowances are to be rated uniformly for the whole building or the whole condominium apartment according to the amount resulting therefrom and to the percentage applicable to the building or the condominium apartment.

(3) If the ownership of a one-family house, a two-family house or a condominium apartment according to subsection 1, is transferred within three years after completion to a natural person, the lawful successor (first acquirer) may take the increased allowances according to subsection 1 in as much as the party

giving the building order has not asserted them. The acquisition costs take the place of the construction costs in the case of the first acquirer. If the party giving the order has not made increased allowances, the year of first acquisition takes the place of the year of completion for the first acquirer. Provided the party giving the building order has made increased allowances, the first acquirer can assert allowances from the year of acquisition at the percentage, and for the period of time, which would have been decisive for the party giving the building order without sale.

(4) If the ownership of a one-family house, a two-family house, or a condominium apartment according to section 1 is transferred within three years after completion via an intermediate acquisition to another acquirer (second acquirer), this second acquirer may take the increased allowances according to subsection 1, inasmuch as neither the party giving the building order, nor the intermediate acquirer have asserted increased allowances for the one-family house, the two-family house or the condominium apartment. For the second acquirer the year of acquisition takes the place of the year of completion. Section 3 sentence 2 applies accordingly.

(5) The increased allowances according to subsection 1 and 2 can already be asserted for partial construction costs.

(6) For the application of subsection 1 to 4 garages belonging to buildings, irrespective of their actual use, are to be treated as serving residential purposes, insofar as not more than one private car for each apartment in the building can be garaged in them. Spaces for the garaging of additional automobiles are always to be treated as not serving residential purposes.

(7) § 7 a subsection 6 of the Income Tax Law is not applicable.

ON § 14 a

Comment I. General Explanations
Comment II. Contents of the Privilege

Comment I

This regulation is concerned in particular with the stimulation of privately financed housing construction in Berlin. The many parallels to § 7 b of the Income Tax Law are intentional and insofar enable an analogous interpretation of both regulations.

The party giving the building order, or in the case of one-family houses, two-family houses and condominium apartments the first acquirer is entitled to the assertion of a claim for this privilege within three years after completion of the privately owned house.

By adding subsection 4 to § 14 a, second acquirers are favoured similar to first acquirers of one- or two-family houses or condominium apartments acquired after November 30, 1974.

With regard to this, the number of privately owned homes a natural person may acquire is not limited.

Comment II

The construction of buildings and condominium apartments which will serve residential purposes by at least 80% for a minimum of three years after their completion is promoted, insofar as no public means have been used to cover the production costs, the current expenses, or the interest on financing funds, or the amortization. Thus, publicly promoted housing construction is not included in this. It is true, however, that the construction of all dwelling houses of this type are favoured, but the size of the dwelling, as well as the expenditure favoured for each is limited. The increased depreciation amounts to 50% of the production costs and can be distributed at will in the year of completion of the building as well as in the following two years. The customary depreciation of such dwelling houses according to German tax law (§ 7 of the Income Tax Law) is 2% annually. The usual depreciation rate is replaced by the special one according to § 7 b of the Income Tax Law.

§ 15 Special Regulations for the Application of § 7 b of the Income Tax Law

(1) For buildings and condominium apartments as well as for their extension, development or reconstruction built in Berlin (West) on a building permit applied for after December 31, 1964,

the regulations of § 7 b of the Income Tax Law in the version of August 15, 1961 (Federal Law Gazette I, p. 1253) remain applicable in a manner that on application depreciation allowances can be deducted from acquisition or construction costs of up to 10% each in the year of completion of the building and the following year, of up to 3% during each of the following 10 years. After these 10 years a depreciation rate of 2.5% of the residual value can be deducted annually until the amortization is completed. § 7 subsection 4 sentence 2 of the Income Tax Law applies accordingly. Instead of § 7 b subsection 1 last sentence of the Income Tax Law in the version of August 15, 1961, the regulations of § 7 b subsection 1 last sentence in the version in effect at the time are applicable.

(2) For buildings and condominium apartments as well as for their extension, development or reconstruction built in Berlin (West) on a building permit applied for prior to January 1, 1965 the regulation of § 7 b of the Income Tax Law are applicable in the version in effect at the time in a manner that depreciation allowances can be deducted from the acquisition or construction costs of up to 10% each in the year of completion of the building and the following year, of up to 3% during each of the following 10 years. Subsection 1 sentence 2 applies accordingly.

(3) If in cases of § 7 b subsection 3 and 4 of the Income Tax Law in the version of August 15, 1961 ownership of a building or condominium apartment is transferred within 12 years after completion via an intermediate acquisition to another acquirer (second acquirer). This second acquirer may deduct the increased allowances according to subsection 1, provided he has acquired the building or condominium apartment after November 30, 1974 and neither the party giving the building order nor the intermediate acquirer have asserted increased allowances for the building or the condominium apartment; for the second acquirer the year of acquisition takes the place of the year of completion.

(4) § 7 a subsection 6 of the Income Tax Law is not applicable.

ON § 15

Comment General Explanations

This special regulation of increased depreciation rates according to § 7 b of the Income Tax Law for buildings and condominium apartments built in Berlin (West) was in existence before it was taken into this Law in 1975; it derives from the equivalent § 53 subsection 3 of the Income Tax Law and opens a higher than normal depreciation rate (up to 50% within 12 years), running on this higher level for a longer period than according to § 14 a. Thus by § 14 a and § 15, every requirement for finance planning is met: high depreciation rates for an extremely short period (§ 14 a) and depreciation rates on a comparatively high level for medium terms (§ 15). The special advantages for buildings in Berlin (West) are to be seen in the two years' 10% rate (West Germany 5%) and the 10 years' 3% rate (West German 2.5%).

§ 16 Tax Reductions for Loans Designed to Finance Investments

(1) For taxpayers liable to unlimited taxation who grant the "Berliner Industriebank Aktiengesellschaft" or the "Niederlassung Berlin der Industriebank Aktiengesellschaft Deutsche Industriebank" a loan under the conditions of subsection 2, the income tax or corporation income tax for the assessment period in which the loan is given is reduced by 12% of the loan given. If the loan has been given from the funds of a business, the income tax or corporation income tax for the assessment period ending in the fiscal year during which the loan was given is reduced.

(2) Requirements for the tax reduction according to subsection 1 are that the loan

1. was given after December 31, 1969
2. according to contractual agreement, must have a term of at least eight years and is repayable at the earliest after the end of the fourth year in amounts not exceeding one-fifth of the amount of the loand and
3. is neither directly nor indirectly in an economic connection with taking up a credit; the availment of current business credits is not detrimental.

The tax reduction according to subsection 1 is granted on condition that a premature repayment of the loan is not made.

(3) The "Berliner Industriebank Aktiengesellschaft" and the

"Niederlassung Berlin der Industriebank Aktiengesellschaft - Deutsche Industriebank" have to pass the loans to enterprises, if necessary by engaging Berlin credit institutes. Those enterprises will use the loans without delay and directly for the acquisition or production of fixed asset items subject to wear and tear of a business establishment located in Berlin (West). The assets must

1. insofar as they form part of the movable fixed assets, remain in a business establishment located in Berlin (West) for a period of at least three years after their acquisition or production,
2. insofar as they form part of the real property of the fixed assets, be built in Berlin (West).

The production of a building in Berlin (West) is equated with the alteration, the extension, the modernization or the repairing of a building in Berlin (West). The "Berliner Industriebank Aktiengesellschaft" and the "Niederlassung Berlin der Industriebank Aktiengesellschaft - Deutsche Industriebank" have to ensure that the loans are used for these purposes only. If the demand for loans for the purposes designated is satisfied, the "Berliner Industriebank Aktiengesellschaft" and the "Niederlassung Berlin der Industriebank Aktiengesellschaft - Deutsche Industriebank" may refuse to conclude any further loan contracts.

(4) The regulations of subsection 1 and 2 are to be applied accordingly to loans given directly to enterprises for the use as designated in subsection 3. For a reduction of the income or corporation income tax in these cases, a further requirement is that the lender and the borrower of the loan agree to a supervision by the "Berliner Industriebank Aktiengesellschaft" and the "Niederlassung Berlin der Industriebank Aktiengesellschaft - Deutsche Industriebank" concerning the use of the loan for the purposes designated, and the performance of the loan contract.

(5) The reduction of the income or corporation income tax according to subsection 1 together with the reduction of the income or corporation income tax according to § 17 may not exceed 50% of the income or corporation income tax that would result without the reduction.

(6) Subsections 1 to 5 do not apply to credit institutes in accordance with the Law on the Credit System of July 10, 1961 (Federal Law Gazette I, p. 881).

§ 17 Tax Reductions for Loans Designed to Finance Building Projects

(1) The income or corporation income tax of taxpayers with unlimited tax liability who grant loans for the promotion of the construction of dwellings in Berlin (West) bearing no interest for a term of at least ten years and dischargeable in equal annual amounts is reduced by 20% of the loans given for the assessment period according to the conditions stated in subsections 3 to 7. If the loans are given from resources of the business by taxpayers ascertaining their profit according to § 4 subsection 1 or § 5 of the Income Tax Law, the loans are to be reflected in the balance sheet at the value resulting after deduction of intermediary interest and taking into consideration the compound interest on the nominal value of the loan. This is to be derived on the basis of an interest rate of no more than 5.5%. Sentences 2 and 3 apply even if the giving of the loan was no occasioned by the business itself. If the loans have been given from resources of a business, the income or corporation income tax of the assessment period in which the fiscal year ends during which the loans were given is reduced.

(2) The income or corporation income tax of taxpayers with unlimited tax liability granting loans on interest with a term of at least twenty-five years for the promotion of the construction, alteration, extension, modernization and repair of buildings in Berlin (West) is reduced for the assessment period of the loan given by 20% of the loan given, provided the requirements of subsections 3 to 7 are met.

Sentence 1 is applicable only if the loans according to contractual agreemtns are

1. to be amortized at the most in equal annual amounts corresponding to the term agreed upon in the loan contract,
2. to bear interest and to be amortized in equal annual amounts under unchanging conditions and, owing to the constant liquidation, the interest-bearing part decreases and the

liquidated part increases correspondingly; changes in the rate of interest for the adjustment to the general level are permissible.

The last sentence of subsection 1 applies accordingly.

(3) A condition for tax reductions according to subsection 1 and 2 is that loans are granted to a party giving a building order and that they are used by this party directly and without delay

1. in the cases stated in subsection 1 for the financing of housing construction in accordance with § 39 or 82 of the Second Housing Construction Law (Housing Construction and Family Dwelling Law),
2. in the cases stated in subsection 2 for the financing of building projects in progress as designated there.

For the application of subsection 1 a further condition is that the loans are in no direct or indirect economic connection with the taking up of a credit. A tax reduction according to subsection 1 and 2 is granted on condition that a premature repayment of the loan is not made; premature repayments after expiration of ten years since the giving of the loan by reason of termination or partial termination by the debtor are, however, not detrimental.

(4) The regulations of subsection 1 are to be applied only insofar as the loans do not exceed 10,000 Deutsche Mark for each flat promoted.

(5) The regulations of subsection 2 and 3 are to be applied accordingly to loans granted to the "Wohnungsbau-Kreditanstalt Berlin" (The Housing Construction Credit Institute Berlin) or the "Berliner Pfandbriefamt" (The Berlin Mortgage Loan Office). The Housing Construction Credit Institute, Berlin or the Berlin Mortgage Loan Office are to pass on the loans, if necessary by calling in Berlin credit institutes, to parties giving the building order who will use the loans directly and without delay for the financing of building projects in progress as designated in subsection 2. The Housing Construction Credit Institute, Berlin and the Berlin Mortgage Loan Office have to make sure that the loans are used for these purposes only. If the demand for loans for the purposes designated is satisfied,

The Housing Construction Credit Institute, Berlin and the Berlin Mortgage Loan Office may refuse to conclude further loan contracts.

(6) The reduction of the income or corporation income tax according to subsection 1 and 2 together with the reduction of the income or corporation income tax according to § 16 may not exceed 50% of the income or corporation income tax that would result without the reductions.

(7) As evidence of the conditions designated in subsection 1 sentence 1, subsection 2, subsection 3 sentence 1, a certificate from the Senator for Building and Housing Affairs or from an authority determined by him is to be presented.

§ 18 Application of §§ 16 and 17 by Workers and Employers

If the income consists totally or partially of earnings originating from dependent work from which a tax deduction is made, and if the conditions of § 46 subsection 1 and 2 of the Income Tax Law do not exist, the assessment for the application of the regulations of §§ 16 and 17 may be applied for; § 46 subsection 2 figure 8 letter a, and subsection 3 and 5 of the Income Tax Law apply accordingly.

ON §§ 16, 17, 18

Comment I. General Explanations
Comment II. The Granting of a Loan Favoured

C o m m e n t I

By means of this regulation, private capital on a larger scale is to be made available to the Berlin economy in the form of outside funds. Only persons with unlimited tax liability who are considered as natives for tax purposes are favoured. Persons with limited tax liability, as a rule foreigners, are not eligible to claim this privilege. Besides natural persons, legal persons (companies limited by shares under German Law, and private limited companies), insofar as they are considered subject to unlimited taxation in Germany, are also entitled to the claim. With regard to loans according to § 16, the tax preference amounts to 12%, on loans according to § 17 it is

20% of the amount of the loan given. The taxpayer may deduct these amounts from the income or corporation income tax debt in the year the loan was given in sums of up to a total of 50% of the tax debt which would have resulted without the reduction. The loans are interest bearing at the usual market rate except those according to § 17 subsection 1.

A premature repayment of the loan within certain periods of time is detrimental to the tax benefit. This means the tax amount originally reduced is subsequently reclaimed.

C o m m e n t II

The loans according to § 16 must be used for industrial investment purposes. Here, too, certain requirements must be satisfied. For example, the movable asset items, as in the case of § 14 subsection 2 No. 1, must remain for at least three years after their production or acquisition in a Berlin business establishment. The loans according to § 17 must be made available for housing construction. The evidence concerning the building project promoted is to be produced by a certificate which is issued by the Housing Construction Credit Institute in Berlin.

By §§ 16 and 17 loans which a shareholder of a corporation grants to his own company are also promoted (see George, Berlin Tax Preferences, 5th edition, p. 207).

§ 18 deals with questions of procedure in the giving of a loan by taxpayers whose income is derived completely from dependent work.

Article III

I n v e s t m e n t G r a n t

§ 19 Investment Grant

(1) Taxpayers according to Income- and Corporation Income Tax Law who have a business or plant (a permanent business establishment) in Berlin (West) can receive an investment grant for assets subject to wear and tear forming part of the fixed assets, and for improvements and extensions of buildings forming part of the fixed assets. In case the assets as well as improvements

and extensions of buildings are acquired or produced by a general or limited partnership according to § 15 subsection 1 No. 2 of the Income Tax Law, the investment grant of sentence 1 is received by the partnership. The investment grant amounts to 10% of the acquisition or production costs of the assets acquired or produced, and the improvements or extensions made in a calendar year. For depreciable fixed assets the investment grant increases

1. to 25% of the acquisition or production costs provided,
   a) the assets directly or indirectly serve production purposes in a plant (permanent business establishment) engaged in manufacturing - except for building industries -
   b) the assets, directly or indirectly serve the production of energy or heat in a plant (permanent business establishment) engaged in power business, including district heating,
2. to 30% of the acquisition or production costs provided, the assets serve exclusively research or development purposes in accordance with § 51 subsection 1 No. 2 letter u sentence 4 of the Income Tax Law.

If the profit is determined on the basis of a fiscal year differing from the calendar year, the fiscal year ending in the calendar year, instead of the calendar year, is decisive.

(2) Investment grants are awarded only for new depreciable fixed assets of a permanent business establishment in Berlin (West) which remain in such a plant (permanent business establishment)for a period of at least three years after their acquisition or production; for ships the period is eight instead of three years.
For passenger cars an investment grant is awarded only if they are used in the enterprise itself exclusively for the conveyance of persons for payment, or for those leased on a self-drive basis, or those used for driving school purposes. For movable assets whoe acquisition or production costs do not exceed DM 800 reduced by an included preliminary turnover tax amount (§ 9 b subsection 1 Income Tax Law) and which are to be independently evaluated and used, no investment grant is awarded. With regard to buildings and to improvements and extensions of buildings, the investment grant is granted only if the build-

ings, improvements and extensions have been carried out in Berlin (West) and comply with the conditions of § 14 subsection 2 No. 2 letter a.

(3) Investment grants can already be awarded for amounts disbursed for prepayments made on the acquisition costs and for partial production costs of assets, improvements and extensions in the calendar year (fiscal year) according to subsection 2. The total amount of the investment grant must also in this case not exceed the percentages of the acquisition or production costs designated in subsection 1. § 7 a subsection 2 sentence 3 to 5 apply accordingly.

(4) After expiration of the calendar year in which the assets, improvements and extensions were acquired or produced, partly or completely, (in a fiscal year differing from the calendar year: after expiration of the calendar year in which the fiscal year ends, during which the assets, improvements and extensions were acquired or produced), the investment allowance will be granted, on application, by the Revenue Office competent for the applicant's taxation on the basis of income from the revenue derived from income or corporation income taxes. The investment grant is awarded to partnerships by the Revenue Office competent for determining the uniform and separate income. The application for the granting of an investment grant can be made only within three months after expiration of the calendar year.

(5) The Revenue Office fixes the investment grant in a written notification. The allowance is due within one month after the date of notification.

(6) If, after the payment of the investment grant, it is noticed that the requirements for the granting of it were either not met or only partially met, the investment grant is to be refunded insofar as it had been unjustly granted. The same applies to assets whose acquisition or production costs were taken into consideration in the assessment of the investment grant and which have not remained in a business (permanent establishment) in Berlin (West) for at least three years (ships for at least eight years) after their acquisition or production. The Revenue Office reclaims the amount in a written notice. A claim for refund of the investment grant arises,

1. if the conditions for granting it have not existed, or have or have only partially existed when the allowance is paid,
2. if assets taken into account have not remained in a place of business or plant (permanent establishment) in Berlin (West) for at least three years (ships for at least eight years) after their acquisition or production when the assets are removed from the place of business or plant (permanent establishment) in Berlin (West).

The claim for refund is to bear interest from that time on when it arises according to § 5 of the Tax Default Law.

(7) The investment grant does not constitute an item of income in accordance with the Income Tax Law. It does not decrease the fiscal costs of acquisition or production.

(8) The regulations of the First and Second Parts of the Reich Impost Ordinance of the Tax Adjustment Law and the Tax Default Law are to be applied accordingly. The claim for refund of the investment grant is barred by limitation after the expiration of five years. Objection to the notifications according to subsection 5 and 6 is permissible.

(9) In public law disputes concerning the Revenue Authorities' administrative documents arising by reason of this article, the stages of appeal for financial affairs are the competent ones.

ON § 19

Comment I. General Explanations
Comment II. Asset Items Eligible for a Grant
Comment III. Amount of the Investment Grant
Comment IV. Investment Grant and the Annual Closing of Accounts

C o m m e n t I

Whereas § 14 with its special depreciation benefit represents especially a financing aid, the investment grant of § 19 is a real tax-free subsidy granted by the State for investments in Berlin. The legal concepts such as assets, business establishments etc. are to be applied hereto as in § 14. The difference first of all lies in the three-month deadline (the application for the disbursement of the investment grant is to be made by March 31st of the calendar year following the year of acquisition or production), as well as in the exclusion of used assets. Every entrepreneur maintaining an operating unit or permanent business establishment in West Berlin is entitled to the investment grant. This applies to persons carrying on an industry, craft or trade, members of the liberal professions etc. Even the legal form of the applicant is of no consequence. Only economic assets forming part of the capital assets and subject to wear and tear are eligible for a grant. It is of no consequence in some special case whether they are actually being used or not. Intangible assets are not eligible. The Revenue Board will fix the investment allowance in a written notification. Of great importance for all problems in this regard is the Circular Order of the Superior Finance Directorate of March 29th (Tax and Customs Gazette Berlin 1971, 321) concerning investment grants.

C o m m e n t II

Only brand new assets forming part of the capital assets are favoured. Assets composed of old and new parts are eligible for the investment grant only if the partial value of the used parts is of relatively minor importance (less than 5%) (Cf. here to the decision of the Finance Court in Berlin of May 26, 1966, decision of Finance Court 1966, p. 449). In case of a general overhauling, the outlay for production costs subject to capitalization is eligible for the grant insofar as the costs concern the costs of acquisition or production of the new parts and the proportion of the assembly costs, and the produced or altered asset has a useful life under usual service conditions of more than 12 months (Circular Order of the Superior Finance Directorate Berlin of September 18, 1967 Tax and Customs Gazette Berlin 1967, 946). The economic asset which has undergone general overhauling must have not only the value of a new one, it must be new in fact.

Today movable assets as well as buildings, enlargements and extensions of premises are eligible for the investment grant. The delimitation is however of importance, because such buildings are entitled to a maximum of 10% (movable assets up to 30%), and even then only if they satisfy the requirements of § 14 subsection 2 No. 2 letter a. Consequently there is a comprehensive court jurisdiction on the question of delimitation. With regard to transportable halls etc., it amounts to determining again and whether there is a solid connection to the ground in the individual case. If there is none, the point of view may be assumed that it is a movable asset. Experience has shown that in such cases it is advantageous to obtain from the Revenue Authorities in good time a confirmation stating that they assess the legal situation as the taxpayer does.

Enlargements and extensions are eligible only if they satisfy the requirements of § 14 subsection 2 No. 2 letter a.

In the case of movable assets, on the other hand, it is required to demonstrate that they form part of the fixed assets of a Berlin business establishment for a period of three years. As in the case of § 14, here, too, all costs of acquisition and production are favoured, including incidental costs of acquisition (transport, assembling etc.), however without turnover tax. In particular cases the Finance Department reserves the right to examine whether in their opinion the acquisition or production costs are considered as excessive. In special cases it is difficult to demonstrate that it is a question of new assets when combined enterprises obtain their machines on the so-called pooling system basis. In that event it is advisable to reach a timely agreement with the competent Revenue Office to avoid unpleasant surprises at some later time. As a rule, passenger cars and assets not subject to capitalization, so-called low value items, i.e. minor movable assets whose costs of acquisition or production do not exceed DM 800 (without turnover tax) are exceptions to the preference of § 19.

C o m m e n t III

The amount of the investment grant for buildings and corresponding enlargements and extensions is 10% of the production costs. Difficulties frequently arise in connection with the delimitation of the so-called processing industry - not including the building industry - because they are paid an increased investment grant of 25% for movable assets subject to wear and tear which are part of the fixed assets, insofar as these assets serve directly or indirectly in the manufacturing process. The concept "processing industry" is to be construed according to general principle. For reason of simplification, the Finance Administration assumes a "processing function" in firms which are listed in section 2 of the Federal Statistical Office's catalogue on sectors of the economy (Tax and Customs Gazette Berlin, 1968, p. 1493). The enumeration in this catalogue is however only an expedient. It is neither the basis for a legal claim, nor does an omission in the catalogue preclude a legal claim. For the investment grant, it is further assumed that assets are used for the most part in manufacturing. Here, too, it is a question of fact as to whether the business assets fulfill a corresponding function in the individual case. Business assets serve production purposes when they are used to obtain the raw materials etc., or if their acquisition or production costs are entered as depreciation in the production overhead charges of the products manufactured by the firm. The administrational-, management- and sales sectors are to be distinguished from the favoured manufacturing one. Assets which do not serve directly the manufacturing sphere are not eligible for a grant. The packing of manufactured goods, if it is done to transport the goods better during the delivery to the customers, is considered as part of the sales process. If, however, according to the prevalent legal opinion, the packing is a composite part of the delivery to the ultimate consumer, e.g. toothpaste in tubes, food in tins, powdered coffee in glasses, margarine in cups, slices of bread or sausage in plastic foil, the packing machines in question serve manufacturing purposes.

With regard to this problem, there is also a relatively comprehensive court jurisdiction, which is constantly being supplemented by new cases of doubt which arise out of the nature of the matter.

The Federal Finance Court decided only in 1970 who was eligible to claim investment grants in leasing contracts concerning movable assets (as well as increased depreciation rates according to § 14). It was stated that the "economic proprietor" may claim for the grant, whoever - lessor or lessee - depending on the kind of contractual relationship is entitled to act as a legal proprietor (see Federal Tax Gazette 1970 II p. 264; George, Berlin Tax Preferences, 5th edition, p. 172). These principles apply accordingly to buildings (see Federal Tax Gazette 1971 II p. 133; George, Berlin Tax Preferences, 5th edition, p. 260).

Investment grants on movable assets acquired or produced for leasing purposes for private use (TV-sets, washing machines, furniture, cars, motorboats) have been restricted by order of the Senator of Finances, Berlin of October 28, 1971 (Tax and Customs Gazette Berlin, 1971, p. 946).

The law has fixed the investment grant for assets serving exclusively research and development at 30%. Legislation has made clear that only such assets are eligible for increased grants that are used exclusively for

a) the gaining of new scientific or technical knowledge and experience of a general nature (basic research) or
b) new development of products or production procedures,
c) further development of products or production procedures, insofar as essential changes in these products or procedures are developed.

The Finance Administration represents the point of view that the assets favoured must remain for three years in the special business sphere (manufacturing or research or development) (Cf. inter alia, the Order by the Senator for Finances of September 19, 1968, Tax and Customs Gazette Berlin, 1968, 1970)

Comment IV

As the investment grant is exempt from taxation, it is of no consequence for the balance sheet for taxation purposes how it is delimited with regard to time periods. It may be included in the final balance of the year concerned as a profit or even in the final balance of the following year in which the notification of the grant was sent. For the balance from a commercial viewpoint, as well as the distribution of profits, it may in some cases be significant to couple the payment to the requirement of the specified three-year period for movable assets. If this requirement is not observed, the investment grant is normally reclaimed.

In conclusion, it is significant that this grant cannot only be received tax-free, but also that it does not reduce the acquisition or production costs, neither in the case of the usual depreciation according to the useful life of the asset, nor with regard to the special depreciation according to § 14 of this law.

§ 20 (Deleted)

S e c t i o n II

TAX REDUCTIONS AND PRIVILEGES FOR WORKERS AND EMPLOYEES

Article IV

I n c o m e T a x (W a g e T a x) a n d C o r p o r a - t i o n I n c o m e T a x

§ 21 Reduction of the Assessed Income Tax and Corporation Income Tax

(1) In the case of persons assessed for income tax
1. who have their sole place of residence in Berlin (West) at the beginning of the assessment period, or who establish it there during the assessment period, or
2. having several places of residence, but have one in Berlin (West) during the entire assessment period and are assessed there, or who have no place of residence in the purview of this law, but have their usual abode in Berlin (West).

The income tax according to tariff (§ 32 a subsection 1 and 5 of the Income Tax Law), is reduced by 30% insofar as income derived from Berlin (West) in accordance with § 23 is concerned. For spouses in accordance with § 26 subsection 1 of the Income Tax Law, it suffices if one of the marriage partners satisfies the requirements of sentence 1. The reduction of the income tax on earnings from dependent work in accordance with § 23 No. 4 letter a is discharged by the supplement according to § 28 subsection 1 sentence 1 received during the assessment period, insofar as the reduction does not exceed the extra pay. Supplements to wages on which wage tax according to § 42a subsection 2 No. 3 of the Income Tax Law is levied by a flat rate are not taken into account.

(2) For corporations, associations of persons and estates having their management and their registered offices exclusively in Berlin (West), the corporation income tax according to tariff (§§ 19 and 19 a subsection 6 Corporation Income Tax Law) is reduced by 20% as far as income from Berlin (West) according to § 23 is concerned, and by 3.2% of earnings contained in the total income from Berlin (West) in accordance with § 23.

(3) With regard to taxpayers, not having met the prerequisites of subsection 1 and 2, who maintain one or several permanent establishments of a business in Berlin (West) and employing a total of at least 25 workers and/or employees regularly during the assessment period, the income tax according to tariff is reduced by 30% or the corporation income tax according to tariff is reduced by 20% as far as the items of income according to § 23 No. 2 are allotted to these permanent business establishments; moreover the corporation income tax according to tariff is reduced by 3.2% of the earnings from Berlin (West) contained in the total income in accordance with § 23 No. 2. If the taxpayer is a co-entrepreneur in accordance with § 15 subsection 1 No. 2 of the Income Tax Law it is adequate if the minimum number of people employed as designated in sentence 1 have been employed in all the business establishments of the enterprise which the taxpayer shares an interest in. If the taxpayer maintains several business establishments engaged in several industries, the reduction is granted only insofar as the minimum number of workers and emplyees, designated in sentence 1 is employed in business establishments of a single industry.

ON § 21

Comment I. General Explanations Concerning the Scope of Privileges

Comment II. Amount of Tax Reductions

C o m m e n t I

Natural persons and corporate bodies are favoured. Natural persons can enjoy these preferences on the following conditions:
1) if the requirements relating to residence according to sub-

section 1 are satisfied (§ 13 Tax Adjustment Law, Federal Finance Court of October 24, 1969; Federal Taxation Gazette 1970 II p. 109);

2) if the person in question has no residence in West Berlin, but has his usual abode there (§ 14 Tax Adjustment Law);
3) if a taxpayer maintains a place of business or a plant of a certain size in West Berlin;
4) if the taxpayer shares in a partnership satisfying the requirements with regard to business establishments in West Berlin as provided by law.

Taxpayers subject to limited taxation, as a rule this includes foreigners, satisfy neither the requirements for having a place of residence nor those of a usual abode. Insofar they have no claim to the tax rate reduction (Administration Court, Berlin, February 28, 1957; Decision of the Finance Court 1957, 357; confirmed by the Federal Finance Court on February 20, 1959).

With regard to individual entrepreneurs' business establishments, or partnerships, the requirements differ. The law requires that "during the tax assessment period an average of twenty-five workers or employees must have been regularly employed". This preference applies to taxpayers subject to unlimited taxation (in relation to taxation, natives) as well as to taxpayers subject to limited taxation (in relation to taxation, foreigners). With regard to a just arrangement which takes into account the situation of taxpayers who establish a new place of business during the assessment period, refer to an order by the Senator for Finance of May 7, 1956 (Section 3 Tax and Customs Gazette, Berlin 1956, 554).

Legal entities (e.g. A.G. or GmbH; companies limited by shares under German law) may enjoy these preferences provided they have either

1) their registered office and management in West Berlin or
2) they maintain a business establishment in West Berlin satisfying the requirements of § 21 subsection 3.

Corporations with foreign shareholders who are assessed for corporation income tax in West Berlin and who have their registered office and management in Berlin (West) (the center of the principal commercial management) are considered as Berlin entrepreneurs. Companies with dual registration of offices (e.g. in Berlin (West) and in the Federal Republic), or foreign stock companies subject to limited taxation can claim these preferences only if they satisfy the requirements of § 21 subsection 3, i.e. by maintaining a business establishment of a corresponding size.

C o m m e n t II

With respect to natural persons, the income tax on earnings from Berlin (West) (§ 23) is reduced by 30%; for corporations the corporation income tax according to tariff is reduced by 20% on earnings from Berlin (West) (§ 23), and by 3.2% on the receipts containing earnings in reference to this.

In the Federal Republic the average tax charge on an income of

DM 100,000	amounts to	43.396%
DM 500,000	amounts to	54.464%
DM 800,000	amounts to	55.999%

Compared with rates in Berlin (West) this presents the following picture:

Taxable Income	Tax Rate in the Federal Republic	Tax Rate in Berlin (West)
DM 100,000	43.396%	30.377%
DM 500,000	53.465%	37.426%
DM 800,000	54.416%	38.091%

There is in addition a trade tax rate on profits which in Berlin (West) amounts to 15% of the trading profits. In the Federal Republic the rate varies locally, but is in general to some extent higher. It is however deductible in any case from taxable profits assessed for income taxation.

A similar situation exists with regard to taxation of legal persons (e.g. A.G., GmbH, Companies limited by shares under German law).

The general corporation income tax in the Federal Republic is
a) 51% on non-distributed profits
b) 15% on distributable dividends.

The same tax rate in Berlin (West) is
a) 37.6% on undistributed profits
b) 8.8% on distributable dividends.

Here the trade tax charge would have to be added too, but this in turn represents a deductible operating expense.

In the case of corporations subject to unlimited taxation, the distribution of profits to be made on the basis of a resolution by shareholders, as provided by the regulations in company law, are considered to be actual distributions.

§ 22 Reduction of the Assessed Income Tax in the Case of Workers Moving In

In the case of workers and employees assessed for the income tax but not meeting the requirements of § 21 subsection 1, who establish their residence in Berlin (West) and take up dependent employment for a continuous period of at least three months, the income tax according to tariff (§ 32 a subsection 1 and 5 of the Income Tax Law), is reduced by 30%, as far as earnings from Berlin (West) are concerned in accordance with § 23 No. 4 letter a. § 21 subsection 1 sentence 3 and 4 applies accordingly.

ON § 22

Comment I. General Explanations

C o m m e n t I

This is of significance only with regard to workers and employees in case of their moving to Berlin (West).

§ 23 Earnings from Berlin (West)

Earnings in accordance with § 21 are

1. earnings from carrying on agriculture or forestry in Berlin (West),
2. earnings realized from gainful activity in a business establishment in Berlin (West). If an enterprise has maintained business establishments (parts of such establishments) in Berlin (West) and other places, the profit of the business establishment in Berlin (West) is considered to be that part of the total profit resulting from the ratio of wages paid to the workers and employees in the business establishment in Berlin (West) to the total amount of wages paid to the workers and employees working in all the business

establishments. The regulations of § 31 of the Trade Tax Law are definitive for the understanding of the term "wages". If there are any pr fits from sales of a whole business entity or a material part thereof in accordance with § 16 of the Income Tax Law, a distribution according to the ratio of the values of the shareholders equity, which are the basis for the calculation of profit from such sales, takes the place of the distribution according to the ratio of the wages;

3. earnings from independent work insofar as they have been realized from work carried out in Berlin (West);
4. earnings from dependent work, if the wages have been
   a) received for work in Berlin (West) from a current employment relationship. If, within the limits of such employment, the wages are received for temporary work outside of Berlin (West), earnings are in conformity with this regulation, provided the workers or employees have their sole place of residence in Berlin (West). For spouses who are both subject to unlimited taxation and who do not live in permanent separation, it suffices if one of the partners has his sole place of residence in Berlin (West). Temporary employment outside Berlin (West) is to be accepted for no longer than twelve months at the longest each time on the occasion of an official journey or an activity limited to a certain period of time or to a limited period of time required to carry out a certain project. Emoluments and benefits derived from previous services rendered which are received together with other wages from current employment from the same employer or from the same public paying department belong to wages from current income in accordance with this regulation;
   b) with reservation to the regulation in letter a, the last sentence, when half pay, retirement pension, orphans and widows allowances or other emoluments and benefits from previous services rendered are received;
5. earnings from investments
   a) in accordance with § 20 subsection 1 No. 1, 2, 4, 5 and 6 of the Income Tax Law, if the taxpayer produces evidence
      aa) that the debtor of such income has his sole place of

residence in Berlin (West) or

bb) that interests are concerned on deposits inclusively loans given to a credit institute with a permanent business establishment in Berlin (West);

b) in accordance with § 20 subsection 1 No. 3 of the Income Tax Law, if the asset items are secured by real estate in Berlin (West), by laws in Berlin (West) subject to regulations of civil law concerning real estate, or by ships that are registered in the Ship Register in Berlin (West);

6. leasing income in accordance with § 21 subsection 1 and 2 of the Income Tax Law, if the real property, copyrights, patents and comparable things or other legally founded claims are situated in Berlin (West) or are entered in a public book or registered in Berlin (West) or have been utilized in a business establishment in Berlin (West);
7. earnings in accordance with § 22 of the Income Tax Law.

ON § 23

Comment I. Distribution of Industrial Income
Comment II. Distribution in Case of Other Income

Comment I

Even if the personal requirements of § 21 have been satisfied, additional proof that the earnings in question have actually come from Berlin (West) is required. With regard to enterprises engaged in trade or industry maintaining several places of business or trade - in Berlin (West) as well as in the Federal Republic - § 23 determines that the aggregate profit is to be divided according to the key of the ratio of wages from Berlin to those wages from the other business establishments. The wages serve as a standard of measure even then if the profit from Berlin can be exactly determined by other means. With respect to this point, the law refers to § 31 of the Trade Tax Law, as the definition of wages contained therein is determinative.

Experience has shown that a problem arises in such cases with respect to the allocation of workers or employees constantly employed outside of town,e.g. sales people (commercial travellers). The business establishment with which the major part of the work performed outside is related is to be considered as the appropriate one for allocation. According to a decision by the Federal Finance Court of November 6, 1956 (Federal Tax Gazette III p. 386), this is as a rule the business establishment from which the outside work was begun and directed. That would mean the salesman's (commercial travellers) aggregate wages are attributed to that place of business from which the travellers' activities are directed, as a rule therefore, the sales department. The sales people (travellers) may thus be attributed to that business establishment where the organization and sales management is situated.

If the total profit contains earnings from business shareholdings, the yields of the holding company are to be treated separately (Federal Finance Court Decision of July 23, 1969, Federal Law Gazette 1969 II, p. 644). When there are profits from the disposition of shares, the division is not made according to the ratio of the wages, but according to the value of the proportionate assets.

C o m m e n t II

Where independent employment and dependent work is involved, the place where the activity is exercised is determinative for the allocation of the earnings. For the allocation of earnings from working for others based on a present employment relationship entailing temporary assignment outside of Berlin, and only temporarily outside, is decisive. With respect to workers and employees engaged by transport and similar enterprises as for example, long-distance truckdrivers, flight personnel etc., it depends on administrational practice whether they are predominantly engaged in Berlin traffic, and can present a Berlin wage tax card. The taxpayer who wants to assert his claim for the preference in the case of receipts from Berlin will have to make inquiries at banks, at the Revenue Authorities, at the Chamber of Industry and Commerce etc. if required.

§ 24 Treatment of Profit-Sharing Business Entities and Affiliated Companies

(1) With regard to the cases mentioned in § 7 a of the Corpora-

tion Tax Law, profit-sharing business entities are to be considered as business establishments of the responsible institution in order to ascertain the items of income realized from trade or business in business establishments in Berlin (West) (§ 23 No. 2).

(2) If there are combinations of an organizational, financial or economic nature in the case of an enterprise with several other enterprises, and the conditions of subsection 1 do not exist, the Revenue Office can for the purpose of reducing the income or corporation tax assess the profit from business or trade of this enterprise on a basis differing from the one used as a basis for assessment of the said taxes. Decisive is the profit which would have resulted according to the conditions of the enterprise without the designated combinations.

ON § 24

Comment I General Explanations

Comment I

If there is a wholly owned subsidiary, recognized for tax purposes, with a profit absorption agreement, the subsidiaries are considered to be business establishments of the responsible body. Even if there is no profit absorption agreement, the Revenue Office may for the purpose of ascertaining the Berlin preference occasionally fix the profit in a manner different from the one used for assessment. The regulation contained in § 24 was devised to counteract abuse. A wholly owned subsidiary exists when a legally independent enterprise in incorporated and subordinated financially, economically and with respect to organization into another independent enterprise.

§ 25 Calculation of the Reduction of the Income and Corporation Income Tax Assessed

(1) If the income consists only of earnings from Berlin (West) or if the total items of income amount to no more than 3,000 Deutsche Mark, the reduction will be granted to the full extent with reservation to subsection 3.

(2) If the income contains other earnings besides those from Berlin (West), the income or corporation income tax is to be

divided up for the calculation of the reduction

1. with respect to taxpayers in accordance with § 21 subsection 1 and 2 in the ration of the total earnings from Berlin (West) - § 23 - to the total amount of earnings,
2. with respect to taxpayers in accordance with § 22 in the ratio of the earnings from dependent work in Berlin (West) which are to be taken into account for the reduction according to this law, to the total amount of the earnings,
3. with respect to taxpayers in accordance with § 21 subsection 3 in the ratio of the industrial earnings which are to be considered for the reduction - § 23 No. 2 - to the total amount of income.

If the amount of earnings not to be taken into account for the reductions of the income or corporation income tax does not exceed 3,000 Deutsche Mark, the reduction will be granted to the full extent with reservation to subsection 3.

(3) If the earnings from Berlin (West) consist exclusively of receipts from dependent work in accordance with § 23 No. 4 letter a, the reduction calculated according to subsection 1 and 2 is granted only insofar as it exceeds the supplements according to § 28 subsection 1 sentence 1 and 2. If the earnings from Berlin (West) consist only partly of receipts from dependent work in accordance with § 23 No. 4 letter a, the reduction in the cases of subsection 1 and of subsection 2 sentence 2 is to be divided up into the ration of the latter receipts to the total amount on income; and in the cases of subsection 2 sentence 1, the reduction is to be divided up into the ration to the total sum of income from Berlin (West). The reduction,which according to this falls upon earnings from dependent work in accordance with § 23 No. 4 letter a, is granted only insofar as it exceeds the supplements according to § 28 subsection 1 sentence 1 and 2.

(4) By statutory order it may be determined that earnings on which the income or corporation income tax is considered as discharged by the deduction will in the case of subsection 2 be left out of account; exemptions, deductions for losses, profits not withdrawn, foreign income or corporation income taxes to be withheld, will be deducted from the earnings to which they are related; additional withdrawals subject to sub-

sequent taxation will be added to the earnings. By the same token, it may be determined by statutory order that in the cases of §§ 34 and 34 b of the Income Tax Law the extraordinary earnings and the income tax falling to their share will be excepted from the division according to subsection 2 or they will be considered separately for the calculation of the reduction according to the principles of subsection 2.

ON § 25

Comment I. General Explanations

C o m m e n t I

This regulates how to proceed with respect to the assessed income and corporation income tax in case the income contains earnings from Berlin (West). For the purposes of calculating the preference in that case, the income or corporation income tax is to be divided up into the same ratio as the earnings from Berlin (West) to the total amount of income. This basis arrangement is then also complemented by earnings, in particular with respect to earnings from dependent work. For further particulars in this regard see George, Berlin Tax Preferences, 5th edition, p. 307.

§ 26 Reduction of Wage Tax

(1) The wage tax falling to the share of earnings from Berlin (West) in accordance with § 23 No. 4 letter b, is reduced by 30% in respect of workers and employees who

a) have their sole place of residence in Berlin (West) at the beginning of the calendar year, or establish it there during the calendar year or
b) having several places of residence, have one place of residence in Berlin (West) during the whole calendar year and reside there for the most part, or
c) having no place of residence in the purview of this law, have their usual abode in Berlin (West).

In respect of spouses who are both subject to unlimted taxation, and who do not live in permanent separation, it suffices for the reduction if one of them satisfies the requirements of No. 1.

(2) If workers and employees destined in subsection 1 undergo the annual adjustment of withholding tax, the tax rate ascertained according to § 42 subsection 4, § 42 a subsection 2 or § 42 b subsection 2 of the Income Tax Law is to be reduced by 30% insofar as earnings according to § 23 No. 4 letter b are concerned.

(3) If workers or employees receive other earnings from dependent work in addition to receipts from Berlin (West) in accordance with § 23 No. 4 letter b, the regulations of § 25 subsection 2 apply accordingly for the calculation of the reduction.

ON § 26

Comment I. General Explanations

C o m m e n t I

This regulation states that earnings from dependent work from which the employer withholds wage tax enjoy the same privilege of 30% deduction as income under the assessed income tax. Pensions and subsistence payments are favoured, however only, if they are paid accordingly to § 23 No. 4 letter b. For preferences with regard to present working conditions see § 28.

§ 27 (Deleted)

Article V

P r i v i l e g e s f o r W o r k e r s a n d E m p l o y e e s i n B e r l i n (W e s t)

§ 28 Privileges by the Granting of Wage Supplements

(1) Workers or employees who receive wages from an occupation in Berlin (West) for present employment (§ 23 No. 4 letter a) will be granted a privilege of wage supplements without detriment to the tax relief according to the regulations of §§ 21, 22 and 26. If the occupation within the framework of the terms of such employment is interrupted or limited, the extra pay will be continued as long as wages are continued to be paid. If in case of interrupted or restricted occupation wages are

not or no longer paid, the extra payment will be continued on a calendar day basis as long as

1. the worker or employee proves to be sick or receives
2. sickness compensation from the official Health Insurance Institution,
3. injury compensation from the official Public Accident Insurance,
4. equalization of income according to § 17 of the Federal Law on Pension,
5. compensation for part-time work or adverse weather conditions,
6. maternity benefits according to the regulations of The Maternity Protection Act or the Reich Insurance Ordinance,
7. temporary benefits during the transition period when measures to maintain, improve or restore the capability to earn a livelihood (therapeutic treatment and occupational promotion) are being carried on,
8. allowance while taking part in occupational education and occupational rehabilitation according to the Work Promotion Law,
9. contribution during an occupational promotion project according to § 26 of the Federal Pension Law,
10. compensation according to the Federal Law on Epidemics, however not exceeding a period of 78 weeks. The wage supplement is granted to workers and employees as well who receive a compensation for loss of wages because of bankruptcy according to the Work Promotion Law; the period workers or employees may claim wages for, which constitutes their claim for compensation, is to be taken into account. This does not apply to periods during which wage supplements have already been granted. The wage supplements are considered neither as taxable receipts in accordance with the Income Tax Law nor as income, earnings of remuneration in accordance with Social Insurance, Unemployment Insurance and Unemployment Relief. Under Labour Law they are not considered as a composite part of wages or salary.

(2) The basis for the assessment of the supplement according to subsection 1 sentence 1 and 2 is the wage received from a current employment relationship (§ 23 No. 4 letter a) for the wage payment period. In the cases of subsection 1 sentence 3,

the basis for assessment of the supplement is the wage for one calendar day of the wage payment period. The wage payment period preceding the interruption or the restriction is determinative; if the employment relationship has just commenced in the current wage payment period, the basis for the assessment of the extra pay is the wage calculated for one calendar day which would be payable to the worker or employee for the determinative, regular period of work without the interruption or restriction. The current wage paid for the wage payment period and other receipts coming in during the wage payment period are considered as the wages for the wage payment period. Not taken into account are receipts on which the wage tax according to § 40 and § 40 b of the Income Tax Law is imposed at a lump sum rate and tax-free bonus for Sunday-, holiday- and night work (§ 3 b of the Income Tax Law).

(3) The assessment basis for the supplement according to subsection 1 sentence 4 are earnings from a current employment relationship, which constitute the claim for compensation for loss of wage because of bankruptcy (§ 141 b, 141 c Work Promotion Law). Subsection 2 sentence 5 is to be applied accordingly.

(4) The assessment basis for the supplement according to subsection 1 sentence 1 and 2 is to be rounded up to an amount divisible by ten leaving no remainder, for monthly wage payment periods; and to an amount divisible by 2.5 leaving no remainder, for weekly wage payments; and to an amount divisible by 0.5 leaving no remainder, for daily wage payments; in the case of other wage payment periods, the assessment basis is derived by multiplying the daily wage by the number of working days and rounding up to an amount divisible by 0.5 leaving no remainder. To determine the number of working days, 2 days are subtracted from each 7 days contained in the number of calendar days in the wage payment period. The assessment basis for the supplement according to subsection 1 sentence 3 is to be rounded up to an amount divisible by 0.5 leaving no remainder,for the supplement according to subsection 1 sentence 4 it is to be rounded up to an amount divisible by 10 leaving no remainder.

(5) The supplement amounts to 8% of the assessment basis inclu-

ding an additional sum for each child noted on the worker's or employee's withholding tax card or a corresponding certification for the payroll period in question. The additional children's allowance for each child amounts to 22 Deutsche Mark monthly, 5 Deutsche Mark weekly or 1 Deutsche Mark daily for workers or employees whose taxes are withheld according to taxation schedules II and III. The additional children's allowance amounts to 1 Deutsche Mark per working day (subsection 4 sentence 2) for other payroll periods than stated in subsection 4 first half sentence.

If taxes are withheld according to taxation schedule IV, the additional children's allowance according to sentence 2 and 3 has to be reduced by 50%.

(6) The employer has to work out the cash supplements and pay them out

1. each time together with the wages in the case of monthly or longer periods of wage payment,
2. in the case of wage payment periods of less than a month, each time for all wage payment periods ending in a calendar month together with the wages for the last wage payment periods ending in the calendar month.

The wages and the supplements are to be separately shown in the wage slips given to the workers and employees. The employer has to deduct the total of the supplements from the amount of wage tax which he has withheld for all his workers and employees, and to set it off in one total sum in the next tax return. If the amount deducted exceeds the total amount of wage tax withheld, the excessive amount will on application be refunded from the wage tax receipts to the employer by the Revenue Office to which the wage tax would have to be remitted. The amounts withdrawn by the employer (sentence 4), the amounts refunded by the Revenue Office (sentence 5), as well as any supplements paid out by the Revenue Office itself reduce the wage tax receipts.

(7) In cases of subsection 1 sentence 4 the competent Labour Exchange Office has to work out the cash supplements and pay them out together with the compensation for loss of wages because of bankruptcy; supplement and compensation payments are to be shown separately in relation to the workers or employees.

On application the supplements paid will be refunded to the Labour Exchange Office from wage tax receipts by that Revenue Office which the employer would have to remit the wage to.

(8) In case the Bankruptcy Commissioner makes out and pays the compensation for loss of wages because of bankruptcy by order of the Labour Exchange Office (§ 141 i of the Work Promotion Law) he has to make out and pay out the supplements as well. The Labour Exchange Office will place means of payment at the Bankruptcy Commissioner's disposal. On request these menas are refunded to the Labour Exchange Office by that Revenue Office which the employer would have to remit the wage tax to.

(9) If supplements according to subsection 1 sentence 3 are not paid by the employer the worker or employee has to prove to the employer that he complies with the requirements for a claim according to subsection 1 sentence 3. Evidence is to be given by vouchers showing that contributions according to subsection 1 sentence 3 are granted. The employer has to note down the nature of the contribution and the period of payment in the wage account.

(10) Claims for supplements are not transferable.

ON § 28

Comment I. General Explanations

C o m m e n t I

This regulation concerns workers or employees who receive wages for employment in Berlin (West) from a present employment relationship. As an additional incentive for an activity of this type in Berlin (West), the State grants a tax-free supplement of 8% of the wage plus a children's allowance of 22 Deutsche Mark per month for each child. This supplement is to be paid monthly to the worker or employee by the employer, who can in turn deduct this sum to the debit of the State from the wage tax which he is obliged to withhold in connection with the monthly payment of wages and salaries and then remit it to the Revenue Office.

To ensure payment to employees who are not in a current employment relationship because of sickness, unemployment, bankruptcy of the employer etc. (see § 28 subsentence 1 Nos. 1 to 10), it is stated that either the Labour Exchange Office or the Bankruptcy Commissioner have to pay out the supplements with the means being refunded by the competent Revenue Office.

§ 29 Supplementary Regulations

(1) The regulations of the First and Second Parts of the Reich Impost Ordinance and the Tax Adjustment Law are to be applied accordingly insofar as nothing else is prescribed in the following subsections.

(2) The worker or employee may apply to the Revenue Office to which the employer has to pay the wage tax or would have to pay in the cases of § 28 subsection 7 and 8 to fix the supplement by written advice. Application is to be made by the expiration of two months after the end of the space of time for which the supplement according to § 28 subsection 6 sentence 2 has to be paid, in cases of § 28 subsection 7 and 8 by the expiration of two months after the compensation for loss of wages because of bankruptcy has been paid. On application the apapointed time may be extended. By written notification the Revenue Office will reclaim any supplements unjustly paid when it discovers that the conditions for the granting of extra pay did not exist. A claim for reclamation arises with the payment of the supplements; it is barred by the statute of limitation after five years.

Protest against the notification in senten 1 and 3 is permissible.

(3) If a supplement has been fixed and becomes legally valid by written notification, the employer is obliged to render payment of the supplement to the worker or employee in accordance with the legally valid notification, provided that the Revenue Office itself does not render payment thereof. The Revenue Office is obliged to send a copy of the legally binding notification to the employer.

(4) The employer is liable for all supplements rendered unjustly. On inquiry by the employer - in cases of § 28 subsection 1 sentence 4 on inquiry of the Labour Exchange Office or the Bankruptcy Commissioner - the Revenue Office has to supply

information regarding the application of the regulations on the granting of wage supplements in individual cases.

(5) The employer has to post supplements rendered according to § 28 subsection 1 sentence 1 to 3 for each wage payment made to the worker's or employee's payroll account or in case no payroll account is kept, he has to enter them separately in corresponding records. In the wage tax vouchers, in the wage tax remittance sheet and in the pay slip, only supplements according to § 28 subsection 1 sentence 1 and 2 are to be especially certified.

(6) Amounts received by the Revenue Office, by reason of evidence connected with the rendering of supplements, especially by reason of reclaiming supplements from the employee or worker, or by making claims on the employer within the limits of his liability, increase the wage tax receipts.

(7) In public law disputes concerning the Revenue Authorities' administrative document arising by reason of this article, the stages of appeal for financial affairs are the competent ones.

ON § 29

This grants the worker or employee the right to have the supplement fixed in a written notification by the Revenue Office. The regulations of the Impost Ordinance and the Tax Adjustment Law apply with the appropriate modifications.

Article VI

A u t h o r i z a t i o n R e g u l a t i o n s

§ 30 Authorization Regulations

(1) The Federal Government, with the approval of the Bundesrat, is authorized

1. to issue statutory orders to carry into effect this article, insofar as this is necessary to maintain uniformity in taxation and in granting of allowances to dispose of injustice in cases of hardship or to simplify administration, namely
   a) with reference to the limitation of the persons favoured,
   b) concerning the ascertainment and limitation of earnings from Berlin (West) including the respective expenditures

and costs in connection with these earnings,

2. to issue regulations by statutory order
   a) with reference to the procedures in granting the subsidies,
   b) with reference to the restitution of subsidies to workers and employees if the total allowances exceed the amount of the total wage tax withheld; a setting off with other levies and contributions made by the employer is permissible. The amounts set off are to be treated as decreases in the wage tax receipt by the Revenue Office,
3. to issue the statutory orders provided for in § 25 subsection 4.

(2) The Federal Minister of Finances is authorized to compile and to publish tables derived from the income tax tables and annual tax adjustment tables for the calculation of the income and wage tax to be reduced according to §§ 21, 22 and 26. In the compiling of the derivation tables the same rounding off is to be employed as in the original tables. The regulations decisive for the general wage tax tables are to be applied to the compilation and publishing of wage tax tables for monthly, weekly and daily payments of wages.

(3) The Federal Minister of Finances is authorized to compile and publish tables for the calculation of extra pay according to § 28 with regard to monthly, weekly and daily payment of wages.

Section III

FINAL REGULATIONS

§ 31 Scope of the Law

(1) As far as nothing else is laid down in the following subsections, the preceding version of this law is applicable for the first time to the assessment period 1975. Sentence 1 applies to tax deductions from wages on the understanding that this version of the law is applicable for the first time to current wages received for a payment period ending after December 31, 1974 and to other emoluments received after December 31, 1974.

Sentence 1 applies to the granting of extra payments according to § 28 on the understanding that the preceding version of this law is applicable for the first time to the wage-settling period ending after December 31, 1974. If the wage-settling period exceeds five weeks, the period of actual wage payment is used instead.

(2) The regulations of §§ 1 to 13 under reserve of subsection 3 to 4 a are to be applied to sales and intrafirm turnover effected after December 31, 1975.

(3) Apart from subsection 2 the regulations of § 4 subsection 1 No. 10 in the version of the Modification Act of the Berlin Promotion Law and other laws from December 19, 1975 (Federal Law Gazette I, p. 3157), the regulations of § 4 subsection 1 No. 15 and subsection 3 No. 5 and 6 are to be applied to sales and intrafirm turnover effected after December 31, 1977.

(4) The consideration agreed upon or charged for scrap iron, junk and waste material including waste by-products has to be reduced in cases of reduction claims according to § 1 subsection 1, § 1 a subsection 1 and § 2 subsection 1

a) by 25% as far as sales and intrafirm turnover performed after December 31, 1975 and before January 1, 1977 are effected,
b) by 50% as far as sales and intrafirm turnover performed after December 31, 1976 and before January 1, 1978 are effected.

The regulations of § 4 subsection 3 sentenc 2 and 3 apply accordingly.

(4a) The consideration agreed upon or charged for roasted coffee (§4 subsection 1 No. 13 letter a) has to be reduced in case of reduction claims according to § 1 subsection 1, § 1 a subsection 1 and § 2 subsection 1 by 50% as far as sales and intrafirm turnover performed after December 31, 1975 and before January 1, 1978 are effected.

(5) The regulations of § 13 a and § 15 are applicable for the first time to the assessment period 1976.

(6) The regulations of § 14 subsection 1 sentence 1 are applicable for the first time to the fiscal year ending after December 31, 1974.

(7) The regulations of § 14 subsection 2 sentence 1 No. 2 letter a and aa are applicable for the first time to buildings con-

structed after December 31, 1975.

(8) The regulations of § 14 subsection 2 sentence 2 first half-sentence and of § 19 subsection 2 sentence 1 and subsection 6 sentence 2 and 4 No. 2 are - as far as the period of eight years is concerned - applicable for the first time to ships, which have been acquired or constructed after May 15, 1973. This does not apply to ships, which have evidently been ordered before May 16, 1973 by the taxpayer or with regard to companies according to § 15 subsection 1 No. 2 of the Income Tax Law by the tax-paying company as well as to ships which the taxpayer started to construct before May 16, 1973.

(9) The regulation of § 14 a subsection 4 are applicable for the first time to one- or two-family houses or condominium apartments which have been acquired by the second acquirer after November 30, 1974.

(10) The regulations of § 16 are applicable for the first time - as far as the words "Niederlassung Berlin der Industriebank Aktiengesellschaft - Deutsche Industriebank -" are concerned from August 6, 1974 onward.

(11) The regulations of § 19 subsection 1 sentence 3 No. 1 are applicable for the first time to movable assets subject to wear and tear produced or acquired after December 31, 1975.

(12) The regulations concerning supplements on compensation for loss of wages because of bankruptcy are applicable for the first time from July 20, 1974 onward.

§ 32 Authorization

The Minister of Finance is authorized to publish the version of the law in effect at the time with the new date, new heading and new sequence of articles thereby avoiding discrepancies in the text.

Section IV

VALIDITY IN BERLIN

§ 33 The Berlin Clause

In accordance with § 12 subsection 1 and § 13 subsection 1 of the Third Transition Law of January 4, 1952 (Federal Law Gazette I, p. 1), this law is valid also in the "Land" of Berlin. Statutory orders issued on the basis of this law are valid also in the "Land" of Berlin according to § 14 of the Third Transition Law.

Bekanntmachung der Neufassung des Berlinförderungsgesetzes

Vom 18. Februar 1976

(BGBl. I S. 353 vom 24. Februar 1976)

Gesetz zur Förderung der Berliner Wirtschaft (Berlinförderungsgesetz — BerlinFG)

Inhaltsübersicht

Abschnitt I

Vergünstigungen bei der Umsatzsteuer und bei den Steuern vom Einkommen und Ertrag, Gewährung einer Investitionszulage

Artikel I

Vergünstigungen bei der Umsatzsteuer §

Artikel II

Vergünstigungen bei den Steuern vom Einkommen und Ertrag

Artikel III §

Abschnitt II

Steuererleichterungen und Arbeitnehmervergünstigungen

Artikel IV

Einkommensteuer (Lohnsteuer) und Körperschaftsteuer

Artikel V

Vergünstigung für Arbeitnehmer in Berlin (West)

Artikel VI

Abschnitt III

Schlußvorschriften

Abschnitt IV

Abschnitt I
Vergünstigungen bei der Umsatzsteuer und bei den Steuern vom Einkommen und Ertrag, Gewährung einer Investitionszulage

Artikel I
Vergünstigungen bei der Umsatzsteuer

§ 1
Kürzungsanspruch des Berliner Unternehmers

(1) Hat ein Berliner Unternehmer an einen westdeutschen Unternehmer Gegenstände geliefert, so ist er berechtigt, die von ihm geschuldete Umsatzsteuer um 4,5 vom Hundert des für diese Gegenstände vereinbarten Entgelts zu kürzen, wenn die Gegenstände in Berlin (West) hergestellt worden sind und aus Berlin (West) in den übrigen Geltungsbereich dieses Gesetzes gelangt sind.

(2) Hat ein Berliner Unternehmer bei einer Werklieferung im übrigen Geltungsbereich dieses Gesetzes an einen westdeutschen Unternehmer in Berlin (West) hergestellte Gegenstände als Teile verwendet, so ist er berechtigt, die von ihm geschuldete Umsatzsteuer um 4,5 vom Hundert des auf diese Gegenstände entfallenden Entgelts zu kürzen, wenn die Gegenstände besonders berechnet worden sind.

(3) Hat ein Berliner Unternehmer Werkleistungen für einen westdeutschen Unternehmer in Berlin (West) ausgeführt, so ist er berechtigt, die von ihm geschuldete Umsatzsteuer um 4,5 vom Hundert des für diese Leistungen vereinbarten Entgelts zu kürzen, wenn die bearbeiteten oder verarbeiteten Gegenstände aus Berlin (West) in den übrigen Geltungsbereich dieses Gesetzes gelangt sind.

(4) Hat ein Berliner Unternehmer an einen westdeutschen Unternehmer Gegenstände vermietet oder verpachtet, so ist er berechtigt, die von ihm geschuldete Umsatzsteuer um 4,5 vom Hundert des für die Überlassung dieser Gegenstände vereinbarten Entgelts zu kürzen, wenn die Gegenstände von dem Berliner Unternehmer nach dem 31. Dezember 1961 in Berlin (West) hergestellt worden sind und im übrigen Geltungsbereich dieses Gesetzes genutzt werden.

(5) Hat ein Berliner Unternehmer Filme, Tonnegative- oder Mischbänder von Synchronfassungen einem westdeutschen Unternehmer zur Auswertung im übrigen Geltungsbereich dieses Gesetzes überlassen, so ist er berechtigt, die von ihm geschuldete Umsatzsteuer um 4,5 vom Hundert des für die Überlassung der Auswertung vereinbarten Entgelts zu kürzen, wenn er die Gegenstände nach dem 31. Dezember 1961 in Berlin (West) hergestellt hat. Auswertung im Sinne des Satzes 1 ist die Überlassung der Gegenstände an Filmtheater und die Ausstrahlung durch Rundfunkanstalten.

(6) Hat ein Berliner Unternehmer für einen westdeutschen Unternehmer eine der folgenden sonstigen Leistungen ausgeführt, so ist er berechtigt, die von ihm geschuldete Umsatzsteuer um 10 [1]) vom Hundert des für diese Leistungen vereinbarten Entgelts zu kürzen·

1. die technische und wirtschaftliche Beratung und Planung für Anlagen außerhalb von Berlin (West) [2]) einschließlich der Anfertigung von Konstruktions-, Kalkulations- und Betriebsunterlagen und der Überwachung der Ausführung, wenn der Unternehmer hierbei ausschließlich oder zum wesentlichen Teil in Berlin (West) tätig geworden ist;
2. die Überlassung von gewerblichen Verfahren, Erfahrungen und Datenverarbeitungsprogrammen, die ausschließlich oder zum wesentlichen Teil in Berlin (West) entwickelt oder gewonnen worden sind;
3. die Datenverarbeitung mit in Berlin (West) installierten Anlagen;
4. die Überlassung von in Berlin (West) selbst hergestellten Entwürfen für Werbezwecke, Modellskizzen und Modefotografien;
5. die üblicherweise und ausschließlich der Werbung oder der Öffentlichkeitsarbeit dienenden sonstigen Leistungen der Werbungsmittler und Werbeagenturen sowie entsprechender Unternehmer der Öffentlichkeitsarbeit, wenn der Unternehmer hierbei ausschließlich oder zum wesentlichen Teil in Berlin (West) tätig geworden ist;
6. die unmittelbar mit dem Betrieb Berliner Film- und Fernsehateliers verbundenen Leistungen für die Herstellung von Bild- und Tonträgern, sofern diese zur Auswertung im übrigen Geltungsbereich dieses Gesetzes bestimmt sind; das gilt nicht für Film- und Fernsehateliers, die von juristischen Personen des öffentlichen Rechts oder in der Form privatrechtlicher Gesellschaften betrieben werden, deren Anteile nur juristischen Personen des öffentlichen Rechts gehören und deren Erträge nur diesen juristischen Personen zufließen;
7. die Überlassung von Vorabdruck- und Nachdruckrechten sowie von Aufführungs-, Sende- und Verfilmungsrechten, auch zur auszugsweisen Verwertung, an den in Berlin (West) selbst verlegten und in Berlin (West) hergestellten Werken;
8. die Auswertung und Überlassung von Informationen und Presseveröffentlichungen durch Zeitungsausschnittbüros.

(7) In den Fällen der Absätze 1 bis 4 erhöht sich der Vomhundertsatz der Kürzung von 4,5 auf 5, wenn die Gegenstände von einem Berliner Unternehmer hergestellt oder die Werkleistungen von

---

[1]) Die Zahl „10" tritt nach der am 1. April 1976 in Kraft tretenden Vorschrift des Artikels 1 Nr. 1 Buchstabe a des Gesetzes zur Änderung des Berlinförderungsgesetzes und anderer Gesetze vom 19. Dezember 1975 (Bundesgesetzbl. I S. 3157) an die Stelle der bisherigen Zahl „6".

[2]) Die Worte „außerhalb von Berlin (West)" treten nach der am 1. April 1976 in Kraft tretenden Vorschrift des Artikels 1 Nr. 1 Buchstabe b des Gesetzes zur Änderung des Berlinförderungsgesetzes und anderer Gesetze vom 19. Dezember 1975 (Bundesgesetzblatt I S. 3157) an die Stelle der bisherigen Worte „im übrigen Geltungsbereich dieses Gesetzes".

einem Berliner Unternehmer ausgeführt worden sind, dessen Berliner Wertschöpfung (§ 6 a) im vorletzten Wirtschaftsjahr mehr als 50 vom Hundert des auf Berlin (West) entfallenden wirtschaftlichen Umsatzes betragen hat; der Vomhundertsatz der Kürzung erhöht sich auf 6, wenn die Berliner Wertschöpfung im vorletzten Wirtschaftsjahr mehr als 65 vom Hundert des auf Berlin (West) entfallenden wirtschaftlichen Umsatzes betragen hat. Die erhöhte Kürzung wird nur auf besonderen Antrag gewährt. Dem Antrag ist eine Berechnung der Berliner Wertschöpfung nach einem vom Bundesminister der Finanzen zu bestimmenden Muster beizufügen.

(8) Die Voraussetzungen für die Kürzungen nach den vorstehenden Absätzen 1 bis 7 sind belegmäßig (§§ 8, 9) und buchmäßig (§ 10) nachzuweisen.

§ 1 a
Kürzungsanspruch für Innenumsätze

(1) Hat ein Unternehmer Gegenstände, die er in einer Betriebstätte in Berlin (West) hergestellt hat, zwecks gewerblicher Verwendung in eine westdeutsche Betriebstätte verbracht und ist ein Kürzungsanspruch nach § 1 nicht gegeben, so ist der Unternehmer berechtigt, die von ihm geschuldete Umsatzsteuer um 6 vom Hundert des Verrechnungsentgelts (§ 7 Abs. 3) für die verbrachten Gegenstände zu kürzen. Die Lieferung der Gegenstände an Abnehmer im übrigen Geltungsbereich dieses Gesetzes, die nicht westdeutscher Unternehmer im Sinne des § 5 Abs. 2 sind, gilt nicht als gewerbliche Verwendung, es sei denn, daß die Gegenstände in der westdeutschen Betriebstätte bearbeitet oder verarbeitet worden sind; die Vorschrift des § 6 Abs. 1 gilt sinngemäß.

(2) Die Voraussetzungen für die Kürzung nach Absatz 1 sind belegmäßig und buchmäßig nachzuweisen.

§ 2
Kürzungsanspruch des westdeutschen Unternehmers

(1) Hat ein westdeutscher Unternehmer von einem Berliner Unternehmer Gegenstände erworben, so ist er berechtigt, die von ihm geschuldete Umsatzsteuer um 4,2 vom Hundert des ihm für diese Gegenstände in Rechnung gestellten Entgelts zu kürzen, wenn die Gegenstände in Berlin (West) hergestellt worden sind und aus Berlin (West) in den übrigen Geltungsbereich dieses Gesetzes gelangt sind.

(2) Hat ein Berliner Unternehmer in Berlin (West) hergestellte Gegenstände bei einer Werklieferung im übrigen Geltungsbereich dieses Gesetzes als Teile verwendet, so ist der auftraggebende westdeutsche Unternehmer berechtigt, die von ihm geschuldete Umsatzsteuer um 4,2 vom Hundert des Entgelts zu kürzen, das auf diese Gegenstände entfällt, wenn die Gegenstände besonders berechnet worden sind.

(3) Hat ein westdeutscher Unternehmer Werkleistungen durch einen Berliner Unternehmer in Berlin (West) ausführen lassen, so ist er berechtigt, die von ihm geschuldete Umsatzsteuer um 4,2 vom Hundert des ihm für diese Leistungen in Rechnung gestellten Entgelts zu kürzen, wenn die bearbeiteten oder verarbeiteten Gegenstände aus Berlin (West) in den übrigen Geltungsbereich dieses Gesetzes gelangt sind.

(4) Hat ein westdeutscher Unternehmer von einem Berliner Unternehmer Gegenstände gemietet oder gepachtet, so ist er berechtigt, die von ihm geschuldete Umsatzsteuer um 4,2 vom Hundert des ihm für die Überlassung dieser Gegenstände in Rechnung gestellten Entgelts zu kürzen, wenn die Gegenstände von dem Berliner Unternehmer nach dem 31. Dezember 1961 in Berlin (West) hergestellt worden sind und im übrigen Geltungsbereich dieses Gesetzes genutzt werden.

(5) Hat ein Berliner Unternehmer Filme, Tonnegative oder Mischbänder von Synchronfassungen einem westdeutschen Unternehmer zur Auswertung im übrigen Geltungsbereich dieses Gesetzes überlassen, so ist der westdeutsche Unternehmer berechtigt, die von ihm geschuldete Umsatzsteuer um 4,2 vom Hundert des ihm für die Überlassung der Auswertung in Rechnung gestellten Entgelts zu kürzen, wenn der Berliner Unternehmer die Gegenstände nach dem 31. Dezember 1961 in Berlin (West) hergestellt hat. Auswertung im Sinne des Satzes 1 ist die Überlassung der Gegenstände an Filmtheater und die Ausstrahlung durch Rundfunkanstalten.

(6) Hat ein Berliner Unternehmer an einen westdeutschen Unternehmer sonstige Leistungen der in § 1 Abs. 6 bezeichneten Art ausgeführt, so ist der auftraggebende westdeutsche Unternehmer berechtigt, die von ihm geschuldete Umsatzsteuer um 4,2 vom Hundert des ihm für diese Leistungen in Rechnung gestellten Entgelts zu kürzen.

(7) Die Voraussetzungen für die Kürzungen nach den vorstehenden Absätzen 1 bis 6 sind belegmäßig (§§ 8, 9) und buchmäßig (§ 10) nachzuweisen.

§ 3
Beschränkung auf den Unternehmensbereich

Die Kürzungen nach den §§ 1 und 2 werden nur gewährt, wenn der Berliner Unternehmer die Lieferungen und sonstigen Leistungen im Rahmen seines Unternehmens und für das Unternehmen des westdeutschen Unternehmers ausgeführt hat. § 5 Abs. 2 Nr. 4 bleibt unberührt.

§ 4
Ausnahmen, Einschränkungen

(1) Die Kürzungen nach § 1 Abs. 1, § 1 a Abs. 1 und § 2 Abs. 1 werden nicht gewährt für die Lieferung, das Verbringen oder den Erwerb folgender Gegenstände:

1. Originalwerke der Plastik, Malerei und Graphik nicht mehr lebender Künstler;
2. Gebrauchtwaren;
3. Antiquitäten;
4. Briefmarken;

5. Edelsteine und Schmucksteine (Halbedelsteine), auch synthetische, sowie Gegenstände in Verbindung mit diesen Steinen, ausgenommen Diamantwerkzeuge (Werkzeuge mit arbeitendem Teil aus Industriediamanten);
6. echte Perlen, einschließlich Zuchtperlen, sowie Gegenstände in Verbindung mit diesen Perlen;
7. Edelmetalle und Edelmetallegierungen in Form von Roh- und Halbmaterial sowie Fertigwaren aus Edelmetallen oder Edelmetallegierungen (hierzu gehören nicht Waren, die mit Edelmetallen oder Edelmetallegierungen überzogen sind);
8. Zinn, Wismut und Cadmium sowie Legierungen, die mehr als 20 vom Hundert Zinn oder mehr als insgesamt 3 vom Hundert Wismut oder Cadmium enthalten, in Form von Roh- und Halbmaterial und von Fertigfabrikaten, außer Druckgußerzeugnissen;
9. Quecksilber;
10. NE-Metalle und NE-Metallegierungen, soweit nicht unter den Nummern 8 und 9 aufgeführt, in Form von Vor- und Rohmaterial, die nicht von einem Berliner Unternehmer durch thermisches Raffinieren oder Legieren in Berlin (West) hergestellt worden sind;
11. Trinkbranntweine im Sinne des Gesetzes über das Branntweinmonopol vom 8. April 1922 (Reichsgesetzbl. I S. 335, 405) in der jeweils geltenden Fassung und Halbfabrikate zur Trinkbranntweinherstellung, ausgenommen Essenzen, die nicht in einer Betriebstätte in Berlin (West) in Behälter bis zu 10 Liter abgefüllt worden sind;
12. Fleisch und genießbarer Schlachtabfall von Rindern, Kälbern, Schweinen und Schafen, frisch, gekühlt oder gefroren; ausgenommen sind
    a) Fleisch und genießbarer Schlachtabfall von Tieren, die in Berlin (West) geschlachtet und in handelsübliche Teile zerlegt worden sind,
    b) Fleisch, das in Berlin (West) durch vollständiges Entbeinen von Köpfen, Schweine-, Kälber- oder Schafhälften sowie von Rindervierteln gewonnen worden ist. Kotelettstränge, Köpfe von Schweinen, Eis- und Spitzbeine von Schweinehälften sowie Köpfe, Füße und Schwänze von Kälber- und Schafhälften brauchen nicht entbeint zu werden. Die Lieferungen und Innenumsätze dieser nicht entbeinten Gegenstände werden nicht begünstigt,
    c) Fleisch aus in Berlin (West) zerlegten Tierkörpern in Einzelpackungen bis zu 1 000 g;
13. a) gerösteter Kaffee (Nr. 09.01 A II des Zolltarifs), soweit nicht sämtliche zu seiner Herstellung erforderlichen Bearbeitungen und Verarbeitungen (ausgenommen Entziehen von Koffein und Reizstoffen) einschließlich der zum Verkauf an Endverbraucher üblichen Verpackung (Einzelpackungen bis zu 500 g) in Berlin (West) ausgeführt werden,
    b) Auszüge und Essenzen aus Kaffee (aus Nr. 21.02 A des Zolltarifs), soweit bei diesen Gegenständen nicht sämtliche zu ihrer Herstellung erforderlichen Bearbeitungen und Verarbeitungen (ausgenommen Entziehen von Koffein und Reizstoffen) in Berlin (West) ausgeführt werden;
14. Zigaretten, Rauchtabak und Zigarren, soweit bei diesen Gegenständen nicht sämtliche zu ihrer Herstellung erforderlichen Bearbeitungen und Verarbeitungen einschließlich der zum Verkauf an Endverbraucher üblichen Verpackung in Berlin (West) ausgeführt werden;
15. Schrott, Alt- und Abfallmaterial einschließlich Bearbeitungsabfälle.

(2) Die Kürzung nach § 2 Abs. 1, soweit nicht bereits nach Absatz 1 ausgeschlossen, wird nicht gewährt für den Erwerb folgender Gegenstände:

1. Rohmassen (Marzipan-, Persipan- und Nougatmassen) und Kernpräparate (geschälte oder zerkleinerte Mandeln, Haselnüsse, Kaschunüsse, Aprikosenkerne, Pfirsichkerne);
2. Trinkbranntweine im Sinne des Gesetzes über das Branntweinmonopol vom 8. April 1922 (Reichsgesetzbl. I S. 335, 405) in der jeweils geltenden Fassung und Halbfabrikate zur Trinkbranntweinherstellung, ausgenommen Essenzen, die in einer Betriebstätte in Berlin (West) in Behälter bis zu 10 Liter abgefüllt worden sind;
3. Fleisch und genießbarer Schlachtabfall, soweit die Gegenstände in Absatz 1 Nr. 12 Buchstabe a, Buchstabe b Satz 1 und Buchstabe c bezeichnet sind.

(3) Soweit nach den Absätzen 1 und 2 eine Kürzung nicht ausgeschlossen ist, ist das Entgelt oder Verrechnungsentgelt zu mindern bei

1. Rohmassen und Kernpräparaten (Absatz 2 Nr. 1) für die Kürzung nach § 1 Abs. 1 um 7 vom Hundert und für die Kürzung nach § 1 a Abs. 1 um 50 vom Hundert;
2. Kupfer und Kupferlegierungen in Form von Vor- und Rohmaterial, wenn die Gegenstände von einem Berliner Unternehmer hergestellt worden sind, dessen Berliner Wertschöpfung (§ 6 a) im vorletzten Wirtschaftsjahr mindestens 10 vom Hundert des auf Berlin (West) entfallenden wirtschaftlichen Umsatzes betragen hat, um 20 vom Hundert, im übrigen um 30 vom Hundert;
3. Trinkbranntweinen und Halbfabrikaten zur Trinkbranntweinherstellung, ausgenommen Essenzen, (Absatz 2 Nr. 2)
    a) für die Kürzung nach § 1 Abs. 1 um 14 vom Hundert, wenn die Gegenstände von einem Berliner Unternehmer hergestellt worden sind, dessen Berliner Wertschöpfung (§ 6 a) im vorletzten Wirtschaftsjahr mehr als 65 vom Hundert des auf Berlin (West) entfallenden wirtschaftlichen Umsatzes betragen hat, im übrigen um 20 vom Hundert,
    b) für die Kürzung nach § 1 a Abs. 1 um 56 vom Hundert;
4. Fleisch und genießbarem Schlachtabfall (Absatz 2 Nr. 3) für die Kürzung nach § 1 Abs. 1 um

30 vom Hundert und für die Kürzung nach § 1 a Abs. 1 um 65 vom Hundert;

5. geröstetem Kaffee (Absatz 1 Nr. 13 Buchstabe a) für die Kürzungen nach § 1 Abs. 1, § 1 a Abs. 1 und § 2 Abs. 1 um 60 vom Hundert;
6. Auszügen und Essenzen aus Kaffee (Absatz 1 Nr. 13 Buchstabe b) für die Kürzungen nach § 1 Abs. 1, § 1 a Abs. 1 und § 2 Abs. 1 um 8,30 DM je Kilogramm, bei Gegenständen in flüssiger Form um 8,30 DM je Kilogramm Trockenmasse, sofern in der Bemessungsgrundlage die Kaffeesteuer enthalten ist;
7. Zigaretten für die Kürzungen nach § 1 Abs. 1 und § 1 a Abs. 1 um 65 vom Hundert und für die Kürzung nach § 2 Abs. 1 um 58 vom Hundert, sofern in der Bemessungsgrundlage die Tabaksteuer enthalten ist;
8. Rauchtabak für die Kürzungen nach § 1 Abs. 1, § 1 a Abs. 1 und § 2 Abs. 1 um 15 vom Hundert, sofern in der Bemessungsgrundlage die Tabaksteuer enthalten ist;
9. den der Werbung oder der Öffentlichkeitsarbeit dienenden sonstigen Leistungen (§ 1 Abs. 6 Nr. 5) für die Kürzungen nach § 1 Abs. 6 und § 2 Abs. 6 um die Entgelte, die an Dritte für die Durchführung der Werbung gezahlt werden.

Die Minderungen des Entgelts oder Verrechnungsentgelts sind buchmäßig (§ 10) nachzuweisen. In den Fällen der Nummern 6 und 9 hat der Berliner Unternehmer in der Rechnung und Rechnungsdurchschrift auch den Betrag anzugeben, um den das Entgelt zu mindern ist.

(4) Die Bundesregierung kann durch Rechtsverordnung mit Zustimmung des Bundesrates bestimmen, daß die Kürzungen nach § 1 Abs. 1, § 1 a Abs. 1 oder § 2 Abs. 1 hinsichtlich bestimmter Gegenstände nicht anzuwenden sind, wenn durch diese Vergünstigungen die Existenz eines maßgeblichen Teils derjenigen westdeutschen Unternehmer erheblich gefährdet würde, die Gegenstände gleicher Art liefern.

§ 5
Berliner Unternehmer, westdeutscher Unternehmer

(1) Berliner Unternehmer im Sinne dieses Gesetzes ist

1. ein Unternehmer, der seine Geschäftsleitung in Berlin (West) hat, auch mit seinen im übrigen Geltungsbereich dieses Gesetzes belegenen Betriebstätten, soweit nicht die Vorschrift des Absatzes 2 Nr. 2 Anwendung findet;
2. eine in Berlin (West) belegene Betriebstätte eines Unternehmers, der seine Geschäftsleitung im übrigen Geltungsbereich dieses Gesetzes oder im Ausland hat.

(2) Westdeutscher Unternehmer im Sinne dieses Gesetzes ist

1. ein Unternehmer, der seine Geschäftsleitung im übrigen Geltungsbereich dieses Gesetzes hat, mit seinen im übrigen Geltungsbereich dieses Gesetzes belegenen Betriebstätten;
2. eine im übrigen Geltungsbereich dieses Gesetzes belegene Betriebstätte eines Berliner Unternehmers, wenn sie das Umsatzgeschäft mit einem anderen Berliner Unternehmer im eigenen Namen abgeschlossen hat;
3. eine im übrigen Geltungsbereich dieses Gesetzes belegene Betriebstätte eines Unternehmers, der seine Geschäftsleitung außerhalb des Geltungsbereichs dieses Gesetzes hat;
4. eine Körperschaft des öffentlichen Rechts und eine politische Partei im übrigen Geltungsbereich dieses Gesetzes, auch wenn die Lieferungen und sonstigen Leistungen nicht für ihr Unternehmen ausgeführt worden sind.

§ 6
Herstellung in Berlin (West)

(1) Eine Herstellung in Berlin (West) liegt vor, wenn durch eine Bearbeitung oder Verarbeitung in Berlin (West) nach der Verkehrsauffassung ein Gegenstand anderer Marktgängigkeit entstanden ist, es sei denn, daß der Gegenstand in Berlin (West) nur geringfügig behandelt worden ist. Kennzeichnen, Umpacken, Umfüllen, Sortieren, das Zusammenstellen von erworbenen Gegenständen zu Sachgesamtheiten und das Anbringen von Steuerzeichen gelten nicht als Bearbeitung oder Verarbeitung.

(2) Weitere Voraussetzung für eine Herstellung in Berlin (West) ist, daß der Gegenstand von einem Berliner Unternehmer bearbeitet oder verarbeitet worden ist, dessen Berliner Wertschöpfung (§ 6 a) im vorletzten Wirtschaftsjahr mindestens 10 vom Hundert des auf Berlin (West) entfallenden wirtschaftlichen Umsatzes betragen hat. Auf die in § 4 Abs. 2 Nr. 3 und Abs. 3 Nr. 2 bezeichneten Gegenstände findet Satz 1 keine Anwendung.

(3) Absatz 2 gilt für Werkleistungen entsprechend. Eine Werkleistung durch einen Berliner Unternehmer liegt auch dann vor, wenn dieser die Werkleistung ganz oder teilweise von einem anderen Berliner Unternehmer ausführen läßt.

(4) Filme gelten als in Berlin (West) hergestellt, wenn die Atelieraufnahmen ausschließlich in Berliner Atelierbetrieben und die technischen Leistungen (Schnitt, Musikaufnahmen, Mischung und Massenkopien) ausschließlich in Berliner filmtechnischen Betrieben durchgeführt worden sind. Tonnegative und Mischbänder von Synchronfassungen gelten als in Berlin (West) hergestellt, wenn die technischen Leistungen ausschließlich in Berlin (West) durchgeführt worden sind.

§ 6 a
Berliner Wertschöpfung

(1) Als Berliner Wertschöpfung im Sinne des § 1 Abs. 7 und des § 6 Abs. 2 gilt der Unterschied zwischen dem wirtschaftlichen Umsatz und dem wirtschaftlichen Materialeinsatz der in Berlin (West) belegenen Betriebstätten des Berliner Unterneh-

mers. Als wirtschaftlicher Umsatz gilt die Leistung des Berliner Unternehmers aus der Herstellung von Gegenständen und aus Werkleistungen in Berlin (West) auf der Grundlage von Verkaufspreisen ohne Umsatzsteuer. Als wirtschaftlicher Materialeinsatz gilt der dem wirtschaftlichen Umsatz zuzurechnende Verbrauch von Roh-, Hilfs- und Betriebsstoffen einschließlich in Anspruch genommener Werkleistungen auf der Grundlage von Anschaffungskosten. Die Tabaksteuer, die Branntweinsteuer und die Kaffeesteuer bleiben bei der Ermittlung der Berliner Wertschöpfung außer Ansatz, soweit sie der Berliner Unternehmer entrichtet hat.

(2) Bei der Ermittlung des wirtschaftlichen Materialeinsatzes kann der Wert der Berliner Vorleistungen wie folgt berücksichtigt werden:

1. Sind im wirtschaftlichen Materialeinsatz Gegenstände enthalten, die ein anderer Unternehmer nachweislich in Berlin (West) hergestellt hat, so können 60 vom Hundert des für diese Gegenstände angesetzten Wertes aus dem wirtschaftlichen Materialeinsatz ausgeschieden werden. Satz 1 gilt nicht für die Gegenstände, für deren Lieferung, Verbringen oder Erwerb nach § 4 Abs. 1 Kürzungen nicht gewährt werden.
2. Sind im wirtschaftlichen Materialeinsatz Werkleistungen enthalten, die ein anderer Unternehmer nachweislich in Berlin (West) ausgeführt hat, so kann der für diese Werkleistungen angesetzte Wert aus dem wirtschaftlichen Materialeinsatz ausgeschieden werden.

(3) Die Bundesregierung kann durch Rechtsverordnung mit Zustimmung des Bundesrates zur Wahrung der Gleichmäßigkeit bei der Besteuerung, zur Beseitigung von Unbilligkeiten in Härtefällen oder zur Vereinfachung des Besteuerungsverfahrens den Umfang des wirtschaftlichen Umsatzes und des wirtschaftlichen Materialeinsatzes näher bestimmen.

§ 7

Bemessungsgrundlage

(1) Zum Entgelt im Sinne dieses Gesetzes gehört nicht die Umsatzsteuer. § 10 Abs. 1 des Umsatzsteuergesetzes ist anzuwenden. Versteuert der Berliner Unternehmer seine Umsätze nach § 19 Abs. 1 des Umsatzsteuergesetzes, so sind die Kürzungen nach den §§ 1 und 2 vom Entgelt zuzüglich der Umsatzsteuer vorzunehmen. Entsprechendes gilt für die Kürzung nach § 13.

(2) In den §§ 1 und 13 treten an die Stelle der vereinbarten Entgelte die vereinnahmten Entgelte, wenn der Unternehmer die Umsatzsteuer nach vereinnahmten Entgelten (§§ 19, 20 des Umsatzsteuergesetzes) berechnet. Anstatt des vereinbarten Entgelts ist das vereinnahmte Entgelt und der Tag der Vereinnahmung buchmäßig nachzuweisen. Bei einem Wechsel der Besteuerungsart dürfen Kürzungsbeträge nicht doppelt in Anspruch genommen werden.

(3) Als Verrechnungsentgelt im Sinne des § 1 a Abs. 1 ist der Betrag anzusetzen, den der Unternehmer hätte aufwenden müssen, um den in die westdeutsche Betriebstätte verbrachten Gegenstand von einem fremden Unternehmer zu erhalten (Marktpreis ohne Umsatzsteuer). Ist ein Verrechnungsentgelt in dieser Weise nicht zu ermitteln, so sind der Kürzung höchstens 115 vom Hundert der nach den einkommensteuerlichen Vorschriften berechneten Herstellungskosten zugrunde zu legen.

§ 8

Ursprungsbescheinigung

(1) Der Nachweis, daß ein Gegenstand in Berlin (West) hergestellt oder eine Werkleistung in Berlin (West) ausgeführt worden ist, ist durch eine Ursprungsbescheinigung zu führen, die der Senator für Wirtschaft, Berlin, auf Antrag des Berliner Unternehmers ausstellt. Der Antrag ist unter Vorlage der Rechnungen oder Lieferscheine zu stellen und mit der Versicherung zu versehen, daß die Voraussetzungen der Herstellung in Berlin (West) (§ 6) erfüllt sind. Die Ursprungsbescheinigung wird dem Antragsteller grundsätzlich in zwei Ausfertigungen erteilt, von denen eine Ausfertigung für den westdeutschen Unternehmer bestimmt ist. Der Senator für Wirtschaft, Berlin, kann Berliner Unternehmern auf Antrag gestatten, die Ursprungsbescheinigung selbst auszustellen.

(2) Absatz 1 gilt entsprechend für die sonstigen Leistungen im Sinne des § 1 Abs. 6 und § 2 Abs. 6.

(3) Der Senator für Wirtschaft, Berlin, bestimmt die Einzelheiten des Verfahrens. Er ist ermächtigt, von den beteiligten Unternehmern Angaben und Unterlagen zur Ermittlung des Tatbestandes sowie über die Höhe der Berliner Wertschöpfung zu verlangen. Die Finanzämter können Auskunft erteilen.

(4) In öffentlich-rechtlichen Streitigkeiten über die Erteilung der Ursprungsbescheinigungen ist der Finanzrechtsweg gegeben.

§ 9

Versendungs- und Beförderungsnachweis

(1) Der Nachweis, daß die in § 1 Abs. 1 bis 3, § 1 a Abs. 1 und § 2 Abs. 1 bis 3 bezeichneten Gegenstände in den übrigen Geltungsbereich dieses Gesetzes gelangt sind, ist durch einen Versendungsbeleg, insbesondere durch Frachtbrief, Posteinlieferungsschein, Konnossement oder deren Doppelstücke, oder durch einen sonstigen handelsüblichen Beleg, insbesondere durch eine Bescheinigung des vom Unternehmer beauftragten Spediteurs, eine Versandbestätigung des Lieferers oder eine Empfangsbestätigung der Betriebstätte oder des Erwerbers oder Auftraggebers im übrigen Geltungsbereich dieses Gesetzes, im Geltungsbereich dieses Gesetzes zu führen. Aus dem sonstigen Beleg muß sich mindestens die handelsübliche Bezeichnung und Menge der Gegenstände, der Tag der Versendung oder Beförderung und das Beförderungsmittel (z. B. Eisenbahn oder Lastkraftwagen) ergeben. Außerdem soll der Beleg die Versicherung des Ausstellers enthalten, daß die Angaben in dem Beleg auf Grund von Geschäftsunterlagen gemacht wurden, die im Geltungsbereich dieses Gesetzes nachprüfbar sind.

(2) Der Nachweis, daß die in § 1 Abs. 4 und 5 bezeichneten Gegenstände im übrigen Geltungsbereich dieses Gesetzes genutzt oder ausgewertet werden, ist durch eine Bescheinigung des westdeutschen Unternehmers zu erbringen, aus der auch der Zeitraum der Nutzung oder Auswertung hervorgehen muß.

(3) Das Finanzamt kann in begründeten Fällen auf Antrag zulassen, daß der Nachweis durch andere Belege geführt wird.

§ 10

Buchmäßiger Nachweis

(1) Die buchmäßig nachzuweisenden Voraussetzungen müssen eindeutig und leicht nachprüfbar aus der Buchführung zu ersehen sein. Die Bücher sind im Geltungsbereich dieses Gesetzes zu führen.

(2) In der Regel sollen aufgezeichnet werden

1. bei den Kürzungen nach § 1:
   a) die Menge und die handelsübliche Bezeichnung der Gegenstände, die geliefert oder im Werklohn bearbeitet oder verarbeitet worden sind,
   b) die Herstellung des Gegenstandes oder die Werkleistung in Berlin (West) unter Hinweis auf die Ursprungsbescheinigung (§ 8),
   c) der Lieferer und der Tag der Lieferung an den Berliner Unternehmer oder der Werkleistende und der Tag der Werkleistung an den Berliner Unternehmer, wenn der Berliner Unternehmer den Gegenstand nicht selbst hergestellt oder selbst bearbeitet oder verarbeitet hat,
   d) die Art der sonstigen Leistung im Sinne des § 1 Abs. 6 unter Hinweis auf die Ursprungsbescheinigung (§ 8),
   e) der Empfänger der Lieferung oder der sonstigen Leistung im übrigen Geltungsbereich dieses Gesetzes nach Namen, Bezeichnung des Gewerbezweigs oder Berufs und Anschrift,
   f) der Tag der Versendung oder der Beförderung des gelieferten oder im Werklohn bearbeiteten oder verarbeiteten Gegenstandes unter Hinweis auf die Versendungsbelege oder die sonstigen Belege (§ 9 Abs. 1),
   g) die Zeit, während der die vermieteten oder verpachteten Gegenstände im übrigen Geltungsbereich dieses Gesetzes genutzt oder die Filme, Tonnegative oder Mischbänder von Synchronfassungen im übrigen Geltungsbereich dieses Gesetzes ausgewertet worden sind, unter Hinweis auf die darüber ausgestellte Bescheinigung des westdeutschen Unternehmers (§ 9 Abs. 2),
   h) in den Fällen des § 1 Abs. 7 die Berechnung der Berliner Wertschöpfung,
   i) in den Fällen des § 6 a Abs. 2 die Art der Berliner Vorleistung unter Hinweis auf die empfangene Rechnung und die Ursprungsbescheinigung (§ 8),
   j) das vereinbarte Entgelt unter Hinweis auf die Rechnungsdurchschrift,
   k) in den Fällen des § 4 Abs. 3 der Betrag, um den das Entgelt zu mindern ist;
2. bei der Kürzung nach § 1 a:
   a) die Menge und die handelsübliche Bezeichnung der Gegenstände, die in die westdeutsche Betriebstätte verbracht worden sind,
   b) die Herstellung der Gegenstände in einer Betriebstätte in Berlin (West) unter Hinweis auf die Ursprungsbescheinigung (§ 8),
   c) der Tag, an dem die Gegenstände in der westdeutschen Betriebstätte eingegangen sind,
   d) der Verwendungszweck,
   e) das Verrechnungsentgelt und die Art der Ermittlung,
   f) in den Fällen des § 4 Abs. 3 der Betrag, um den das Verrechnungsentgelt zu mindern ist;
3. bei den Kürzungen nach § 2:
   a) die Menge und die handelsübliche Bezeichnung der Gegenstände, die erworben oder im Werklohn bearbeitet oder verarbeitet worden sind,
   b) der Lieferer oder der Leistende,
   c) der Ort der Herstellung oder der Werkleistung unter Hinweis auf die Ursprungsbescheinigung (§ 8),
   d) die Art der sonstigen Leistung im Sinne des § 2 Abs. 6 unter Hinweis auf die Ursprungsbescheinigung (§ 8),
   e) der Tag des Empfangs der Gegenstände im übrigen Geltungsbereich dieses Gesetzes unter Hinweis auf den Frachtbrief oder andere Belege,
   f) die Zeit, während der die gemieteten oder gepachteten Gegenstände im übrigen Geltungsbereich dieses Gesetzes genutzt oder die Filme, Tonnegative oder Mischbänder von Synchronfassungen im übrigen Geltungsbereich dieses Gesetzes ausgewertet worden sind,
   g) das vereinbarte Entgelt unter Hinweis auf die empfangene Rechnung,
   h) in den Fällen des § 4 Abs. 3 der Betrag, um den das Entgelt zu mindern ist.

(3) Das Finanzamt kann einem steuerlich zuverlässigen Unternehmer gestatten, daß er den buchmäßigen Nachweis in anderer Weise erbringt.

§ 11

Verfahren bei der Kürzung

(1) Die Kürzungsbeträge nach den §§ 1, 1 a und 2 sind mit der für einen Voranmeldungszeitraum oder Veranlagungszeitraum geschuldeten Umsatzsteuer zu verrechnen. § 18 Abs. 2 Satz 4 und 5 und Abs. 4 Satz 4 des Umsatzsteuergesetzes ist anzuwenden.

(2) Werden Entgelte oder Verrechnungsentgelte gemindert, so sind Kürzungsbeträge nach den §§ 1, 1 a und 2 insoweit zurückzuzahlen, als diese auf die Entgeltminderung entfallen. Der zurückzuzahlende Betrag ist der Steuerschuld für den Voranmeldungszeitraum (Veranlagungszeitraum) hinzuzurechnen, in dem die Entgelte gemindert werden.

(3) Absatz 2 gilt sinngemäß, wenn vereinbarte Entgelte uneinbringlich geworden sind. Werden die Entgelte nachträglich vereinnahmt, kann der Unternehmer die Kürzung der Umsatzsteuer erneut vornehmen.

§ 12

Wegfall der Kürzungsansprüche

Gelangen Gegenstände, für deren Verbringen oder Erwerb Anspruch auf die Kürzungen nach § 1 a oder § 2 besteht, nach Berlin (West) zurück, ohne daß die Gegenstände im übrigen Geltungsbereich dieses Gesetzes einer Bearbeitung oder Verarbeitung im Sinne des § 6 Abs. 1 unterlegen haben, so darf die Kürzung der geschuldeten Umsatzsteuer nicht vorgenommen werden. Liefert der westdeutsche Unternehmer die Gegenstände an den Berliner Lieferer zurück, so darf auch die Kürzung nach § 1 nicht vorgenommen werden. Ist die Kürzung bereits vorgenommen worden, so ist der Kürzungsbetrag an das Finanzamt zurückzuzahlen.

§ 13

Besonderer Kürzungsanspruch für Unternehmer in Berlin (West)

(1) Unternehmer, für deren Besteuerung nach dem Umsatz ein Finanzamt in Berlin (West) zuständig ist (§ 73 Abs. 4 der Reichsabgabenordnung) und deren Gesamtumsatz (§ 19 Abs. 3 des Umsatzsteuergesetzes) im laufenden Kalenderjahr 200 000 Deutsche Mark nicht übersteigt, sind unbeschadet der Kürzungen nach den §§ 1, 1 a und 2 berechtigt, die Umsatzsteuer, die sie für einen Voranmeldungszeitraum (Veranlagungszeitraum) schulden, um 4 vom Hundert des Entgelts für ihre im gleichen Zeitraum bewirkten steuerpflichtigen Umsätze zu kürzen. Der Kürzungsbetrag darf 720 Deutsche Mark im Kalenderjahr nicht übersteigen. Sind im Gesamtumsatz lediglich Umsätze aus freiberuflicher Tätigkeit im Sinne des § 18 Abs. 1 Ziff. 1 des Einkommensteuergesetzes oder aus einer Tätigkeit als Handelsvertreter oder Makler enthalten, so beträgt der Kürzungsbetrag höchstens 1 200 Deutsche Mark im Kalenderjahr. § 18 Abs. 2 Satz 4 und 5 und Abs. 4 Satz 4 des Umsatzsteuergesetzes ist anzuwenden.

(2) Sind im Gesamtumsatz sowohl Umsätze aus freiberuflicher Tätigkeit oder aus einer Tätigkeit als Handelsvertreter oder Makler als auch andere Umsätze enthalten, so kann hinsichtlich der erstgenannten Umsätze die Kürzung bis zur Höhe von 1 200 Deutsche Mark vorgenommen werden. Ergibt sich bei diesen Umsätzen ein niedrigerer Kürzungsbetrag als 1 200 Deutsche Mark, so kann der nicht verbrauchte Rest des Kürzungsbetrages von 1 200 Deutsche Mark bis zu einem Höchstbetrag von 720 Deutsche Mark von der für die anderen Umsätze geschuldeten Umsatzsteuer abgesetzt werden.

(3) Unternehmer im Sinne des Absatzes 1, deren Gesamtumsatz im laufenden Kalenderjahr 200 000 Deutsche Mark übersteigt, können von ihrer Umsatzsteuerschuld einen Betrag absetzen, dessen Höhe wie folgt zu berechnen ist:

Der Betrag, der bei Nichtberücksichtigung der Umsatzgrenze von 200 000 Deutsche Mark absetzbar wäre, wird um 4 vom Hundert des Betrages gekürzt, um den der Gesamtumsatz höher ist als 200 000 Deutsche Mark.

Artikel II

Vergünstigungen bei den Steuern vom Einkommen und Ertrag

§ 13 a

Sondervorschriften zur Anwendung des § 6 a und des § 7 Abs. 2 des Einkommensteuergesetzes

(1) Bei der Berechnung des Teilwerts einer Pensionsverpflichtung ist abweichend von § 6 a Abs. 3 letzter Satz des Einkommensteuergesetzes ein Rechnungszinsfuß von mindestens 3,5 vom Hundert anzuwenden, wenn der Pensionsberechtigte

1. bei einer Pensionsrückstellung vor Beendigung des Dienstverhältnisses des Pensionsberechtigten in dem betreffenden Wirtschaftsjahr,
2. bei einer Pensionsrückstellung nach Beendigung des Dienstverhältnisses des Pensionsberechtigten unter Aufrechterhaltung seiner Pensionsanwartschaft oder nach Eintritt des Versorgungsfalles

   in dem letzten Wirtschaftsjahr vor der Beendigung des Dienstverhältnisses oder dem Eintritt des Versorgungsfalles

mindestens acht Monate in einer in Berlin (West) belegenen Betriebstätte beschäftigt war.

(2) Bei beweglichen Wirtschaftsgütern, die zum Anlagevermögen einer in Berlin (West) belegenen Betriebstätte gehören und mindestens drei Jahre nach ihrer Anschaffung oder Herstellung in einer solchen Betriebstätte verbleiben, ist § 7 Abs. 2 Satz 2 des Einkommensteuergesetzes 1958 (Bundesgesetzbl. I S.672)[1] weiter anzuwenden.

§ 14

Erhöhte Absetzungen für abnutzbare Wirtschaftsgüter des Anlagevermögens

(1) Bei abnutzbaren Wirtschaftsgütern, die zum Anlagevermögen einer in Berlin (West) belegenen Betriebstätte gehören und bei denen die Voraussetzungen des Absatzes 2 vorliegen, können im Wirtschaftsjahr der Anschaffung oder Herstellung und in den vier folgenden Wirtschaftsjahren an Stelle der nach § 7 des Einkommensteuergesetzes zu bemessenden Absetzungen für Abnutzung erhöhte Absetzungen bis zur Höhe von insgesamt 75 vom Hundert der Anschaffungs- oder Herstellungskosten vorgenommen werden. Von dem Wirtschaftsjahr an, in dem erhöhte Absetzungen nach Satz 1 nicht mehr vorgenommen werden können, spätestens vom fünften auf das Wirtschaftsjahr der Anschaffung oder Herstellung folgenden Wirtschaftsjahr an, sind die Absetzungen für Abnutzung bei beweglichen Wirtschaftsgütern in gleichen Jahresbeträgen nach dem Restwert und der Restnutzungsdauer, bei Gebäuden nach dem Restwert und dem nach § 7 Abs. 4 des

[1]) GVBl. S. 993

Einkommensteuergesetzes unter Berücksichtigung der Restnutzungsdauer maßgebenden Hundertsatz zu bemessen.

(2) Die erhöhten Absetzungen nach Absatz 1 können in Anspruch genommen werden

1. für bewegliche Wirtschaftsgüter, die mindestens drei Jahre nach ihrer Anschaffung oder Herstellung in einer in Berlin (West) belegenen Betriebstätte verbleiben;
2. für Gebäude, die in Berlin (West) errichtet werden und
   a) im eigenen gewerblichen Betrieb zu mehr als 80 vom Hundert unmittelbar
      aa) der Fertigung von zum Absatz bestimmten Wirtschaftsgütern oder der Erzeugung von Energie oder Wärme oder
      bb) der Bearbeitung von zum Absatz bestimmten Wirtschaftsgütern oder
      cc) der Wiederherstellung von Wirtschaftsgütern oder
      dd) der Forschung oder Entwicklung im Sinne des § 51 Abs. 1 Ziff. 2 Buchstabe u Satz 4 des Einkommensteuergesetzes oder
      ee) der Geschäftsführung oder Verwaltung oder der Lagerung von Vorräten im Zusammenhang mit den in den Doppelbuchstaben aa bis dd bezeichneten Tätigkeiten

   oder
   b) zu mehr als 80 vom Hundert Angehörigen des eigenen gewerblichen Betriebs zu Wohnzwekken

   dienen. Bei Schiffen ist die Vorschrift des Satzes 1 Nr. 1 mit der Maßgabe anzuwenden, daß an die Stelle des Zeitraums von drei Jahren ein Zeitraum von acht Jahren tritt; im Falle der Anschaffung eines Schiffs ist weitere Voraussetzung für die Anwendung des Absatzes 1, daß das Schiff in ungebrauchtem Zustand vom Hersteller erworben worden ist.

(3) Die erhöhten Absetzungen nach Absatz 1 können auch für Ausbauten und Erweiterungen an bestehenden Gebäuden in Anspruch genommen werden, wenn die ausgebauten oder neu hergestellten Gebäudeteile die Voraussetzungen des Absatzes 2 Nr. 2 erfüllen. Die erhöhten Absetzungen bemessen sich in diesem Fall nach den Herstellungskosten, die für den Ausbau oder die Erweiterung aufgewendet worden sind. Von dem Wirtschaftsjahr an, in dem erhöhte Absetzungen nach Satz 1 nicht mehr vorgenommen werden können, ist der Restwert den Anschaffungs- oder Herstellungskosten des Gebäudes oder dem an deren Stelle tretenden Wert hinzuzurechnen; die weiteren Absetzungen für Abnutzung sind einheitlich für das gesamte Gebäude nach dem sich hiernach ergebenden Betrag und dem für das Gebäude maßgebenden Hundertsatz zu bemessen.

(4) Die erhöhten Absetzungen nach den Absätzen 1 und 3 können bereits für Anzahlungen auf Anschaffungskosten und für Teilherstellungskosten in Anspruch genommen werden.

(5) § 7 a Abs. 6 des Einkommensteuergesetzes ist nicht anzuwenden.

(6) Auf Gebäude, mit deren Herstellung vor dem 1. Januar 1970 begonnen worden ist und die vor dem 1. Januar 1975 fertiggestellt werden, sind die Vorschriften des § 14 des Berlinhilfegesetzes in der Fassung der Bekanntmachung vom 19. August 1964 (Bundesgesetzbl. I S. 674)[8] weiter anzuwenden.

§ 14 a
Erhöhte Absetzungen für Wohngebäude und Eigentumswohnungen

(1) Bei Gebäuden und Eigentumswohnungen, die im steuerbegünstigten oder frei finanzierten Wohnungsbau in Berlin (West) hergestellt worden sind und die mindestens drei Jahre nach ihrer Fertigstellung zu mehr als 80 vom Hundert Wohnzwecken dienen, kann der Bauherr abweichend von § 7 Abs. 4 und 5 des Einkommensteuergesetzes im Jahr der Fertigstellung des Gebäudes und in den beiden folgenden Jahren erhöhte Absetzungen bis zur Höhe von insgesamt 50 vom Hundert der Herstellungskosten vornehmen. Von dem Jahr an, in dem erhöhte Absetzungen nach Satz 1 nicht mehr vorgenommen werden können, spätestens vom dritten auf das Jahr der Fertigstellung folgenden Jahr an, sind die Absetzungen für Abnutzung nach dem Restwert und dem nach § 7 Abs. 4 des Einkommensteuergesetzes unter Berücksichtigung der Restnutzungsdauer maßgebenden Hundertsatz zu bemessen. Übersteigen die Herstellungskosten bei einem Einfamilienhaus oder einer Eigentumswohnung die Grenze von 150 000 Deutsche Mark, bei einem Zweifamilienhaus die Grenze von 200 000 Deutsche Mark, so sind auf den übersteigenden Teil der Herstellungskosten die Vorschriften des § 7 Abs. 4 des Einkommensteuergesetzes anzuwenden.

(2) Die erhöhten Absetzungen nach Absatz 1 Satz 1 können auch für Ausbauten und Erweiterungen an Gebäuden und Eigentumswohnungen in Berlin (West) in Anspruch genommen werden, wenn die Ausbauten oder Erweiterungen im steuerbegünstigten oder frei finanzierten Wohnungsbau hergestellt worden sind und die ausgebauten oder neu hergestellten Gebäudeteile mindestens drei Jahre nach ihrer Fertigstellung zu mehr als 80 vom Hundert Wohnzwecken dienen. Die erhöhten Absetzungen bemessen sich in diesem Fall nach den Herstellungskosten, die für den Ausbau oder die Erweiterung aufgewendet worden sind. Absatz 1 Satz 3 gilt entsprechend. Von dem Jahr an, in dem erhöhte Absetzungen nach Satz 1 nicht mehr vorgenommen werden können, ist der Restwert den Anschaffungs- oder Herstellungskosten des Gebäudes oder der Eigentumswohnung oder dem an deren Stelle tretenden Wert hinzuzurechnen; die weiteren Absetzungen für Abnutzung sind einheitlich für das gesamte Gebäude oder die gesamte Eigentumswohnung nach dem sich hiernach ergebenden Betrag und dem für das Gebäude oder die Eigentumswohnung maßgebenden Hundertsatz zu bemessen.

[8] GVBl. S. 994

(3) Geht das Eigentum an einem Einfamilienhaus, einem Zweifamilienhaus oder einer Eigentumswohnung im Sinne des Absatzes 1 innerhalb von drei Jahren nach der Fertigstellung auf eine natürliche Person über, so kann der Rechtsnachfolger (Ersterwerber) die erhöhten Absetzungen im Sinne des Absatzes 1 vornehmen, soweit der Bauherr sie nicht geltend gemacht hat. Für den Ersterwerber treten an die Stelle der Herstellungskosten die Anschaffungskosten. Hat der Bauherr keine erhöhten Absetzungen vorgenommen, so tritt für den Ersterwerber an die Stelle des Jahres der Fertigstellung das Jahr des Ersterwerbs. Hat der Bauherr erhöhte Absetzungen vorgenommen, so kann der Ersterwerber sie vom Jahr des Ersterwerbs an mit dem Hundertsatz und für den Zeitraum geltend machen, die für den Bauherrn ohne die Veräußerung maßgebend gewesen wären.

(4) Geht das Eigentum an einem Einfamilienhaus, einem Zweifamilienhaus oder einer Eigentumswohnung im Sinne des Absatzes 1 innerhalb von drei Jahren nach Fertigstellung nach einem Zwischenerwerb auf einen neuen Erwerber (Zweiterwerber) über, so kann der Zweiterwerber die erhöhten Absetzungen im Sinne des Absatzes 1 vornehmen, wenn weder der Bauherr noch der Zwischenerwerber für das Einfamilienhaus, das Zweifamilienhaus oder die Eigentumswohnung erhöhte Absetzungen geltend gemacht hat. Für den Zweiterwerber tritt an die Stelle des Jahres der Fertigstellung das Jahr des Zweiterwerbs. Absatz 3 Satz 2 gilt entsprechend.

(5) Die erhöhten Absetzungen nach den Absätzen 1 und 2 können bereits für Teilherstellungskosten in Anspruch genommen werden.

(6) Für die Anwendung der Absätze 1 bis 4 sind zum Gebäude gehörende Garagen ohne Rücksicht auf ihre tatsächliche Nutzung als Wohnzwecken dienend zu behandeln, soweit in ihnen nicht mehr als ein Personenkraftwagen für jede in dem Gebäude befindliche Wohnung untergestellt werden kann. Räume für die Unterstellung weiterer Kraftwagen sind stets als nicht Wohnzwecken dienend zu behandeln.

(7) § 7 a Abs. 6 des Einkommensteuergesetzes ist nicht anzuwenden.

§ 15

Sondervorschriften zur Anwendung des § 7 b des Einkommensteuergesetzes

(1) Bei Gebäuden und Eigentumswohnungen sowie bei Zubauten, Ausbauten und Umbauten, die in Berlin (West) errichtet worden sind und bei denen der Antrag auf Baugenehmigung nach dem 31. Dezember 1964 gestellt worden ist, sind die Vorschriften des § 7 b des Einkommensteuergesetzes in der Fassung der Bekanntmachung vom 15. August 1961 (Bundesgesetzbl. I S. 1253)[9] mit der Maßgabe weiter anzuwenden, daß auf Antrag im Jahr der Fertigstellung und in dem darauffolgenden Jahr jeweils bis zu 10 vom Hundert, ferner in den darauffolgenden zehn Jahren jeweils bis zu 3 vom Hundert der Anschaffungs- oder Herstellungskosten abgesetzt werden können. Nach Ablauf dieser zehn Jahre sind als Absetzung für Abnutzung bis zur vollen Absetzung jährlich 2,5 vom Hundert des Restwerts abzuziehen; § 7 Abs. 4 Satz 2 des Einkommensteuergesetzes gilt entsprechend. An Stelle der Vorschrift des § 7 b Abs. 1 letzter Satz des Einkommensteuergesetzes in der Fassung vom 15. August 1961 ist die Vorschrift des § 7 b Abs. 1 letzter Satz des Einkommensteuergesetzes in der jeweils geltenden Fassung anzuwenden.

(2) Bei Gebäuden und Eigentumswohnungen sowie bei Zubauten, Ausbauten und Umbauten, die in Berlin (West) errichtet worden sind und bei denen der Antrag auf Baugenehmigung vor dem 1. Januar 1965 gestellt worden ist, sind die Vorschriften des § 7 b des Einkommensteuergesetzes in der jeweils geltenden Fassung mit der Maßgabe anzuwenden, daß im Jahr der Fertigstellung und in dem darauffolgenden Jahr jeweils bis zu 10 vom Hundert, ferner in den darauffolgenden zehn Jahren jeweils bis zu 3 vom Hundert der Anschaffungs- oder Herstellungskosten abgesetzt werden können. Absatz 1 Satz 2 gilt entsprechend.

(3) Geht in den Fällen des § 7 b Abs. 3 und 4 des Einkommensteuergesetzes in der Fassung vom 15. August 1961 das Gebäude oder die Eigentumswohnung innerhalb von zwölf Jahren nach Fertigstellung nach einem Zwischenerwerb auf einen neuen Erwerber (Zweiterwerber) über, so kann der Zweiterwerber die erhöhten Absetzungen nach Absatz 1 vornehmen, wenn er das Gebäude oder die Eigentumswohnung nach dem 30. November 1974 angeschafft hat und weder der Bauherr noch der Zwischenerwerber für das Gebäude oder die Eigentumswohnung erhöhte Absetzungen geltend gemacht hat; für den Zweiterwerber treten an die Stelle des Jahres der Fertigstellung das Jahr des Zweiterwerbs und an die Stelle der Herstellungskosten die Anschaffungskosten.

(4) § 7 a Abs. 6 des Einkommensteuergesetzes ist nicht anzuwenden.

§ 16

Steuerermäßigung für Darlehen zur Finanzierung von betrieblichen Investitionen

(1) Bei unbeschränkt Steuerpflichtigen, die der Berliner Industriebank Aktiengesellschaft oder der Niederlassung Berlin der Industriekreditbank Aktiengesellschaft — Deutsche Industriebank unter den Voraussetzungen des Absatzes 2 Darlehen gewähren, ermäßigt sich die Einkommensteuer oder Körperschaftsteuer für den Veranlagungszeitraum der Hingabe um zwölf vom Hundert der hingegebenen Darlehen. Sind die Darlehen aus Mitteln eines Betriebs gegeben worden, so ermäßigt sich die Einkommensteuer oder Körperschaftsteuer des Veranlagungszeitraums, in dem das Wirtschaftsjahr endet, in dessen Verlauf die Darlehen gegeben worden sind.

(2) Voraussetzung für die Steuerermäßigung nach Absatz 1 ist, daß die Darlehen

1. nach dem 31. Dezember 1969 hingegeben werden,
2. nach den vertraglichen Vereinbarungen eine Laufzeit von mindestens acht Jahren haben und frühestens vom Ende des vierten Jahres an jähr-

[9]) GVBl. S. 1251

lich mit höchstens einem Fünftel des Darlehnsbetrags zurückzuzahlen sind und

3. weder unmittelbar noch mittelbar in wirtschaftlichem Zusammenhang mit der Aufnahme eines Kredits stehen; die Inanspruchnahme laufender Geschäftskredite ist unschädlich.

Die Steuerermäßigung nach Absatz 1 wird unter der Bedingung gewährt, daß eine vorzeitige Rückzahlung der Darlehen nicht stattfindet.

(3) Die Berliner Industriebank Aktiengesellschaft und die Niederlassung Berlin der Industriekreditbank Aktiengesellschaft — Deutsche Industriebank haben die Darlehen, gegebenenfalls unter Einschaltung von Berliner Kreditinstituten, an Unternehmen weiterzugeben, die die Darlehen unverzüglich und unmittelbar zur Anschaffung oder Herstellung abnutzbarer Wirtschaftsgüter des Anlagevermögens einer in Berlin (West) belegenen Betriebstätte verwenden. Die Wirtschaftsgüter müssen,

1. soweit sie zum beweglichen Anlagevermögen gehören, mindestens drei Jahre nach ihrer Anschaffung oder Herstellung in einer in Berlin (West) belegenen Betriebstätte verbleiben,
2. soweit sie zum unbeweglichen Anlagevermögen gehören, in Berlin (West) errichtet werden.

Der Herstellung eines Gebäudes in Berlin (West) steht der Umbau, die Erweiterung, die Modernisierung oder die Instandsetzung eines Gebäudes in Berlin (West) gleich. Die Berliner Industriebank Aktiengesellschaft und die Niederlassung Berlin der Industriekreditbank Aktiengesellschaft — Deutsche Industriebank haben sicherzustellen, daß die Darlehen nur zu diesen Zwecken verwendet werden. Ist der Bedarf an Darlehen für die bezeichneten Zwecke gedeckt, so können die Berliner Industriebank Aktiengesellschaft und die Niederlassung Berlin der Industriekreditbank Aktiengesellschaft — Deutsche Industriebank den Abschluß weiterer Darlehensverträge ablehnen.

(4) Die Vorschriften der Absätze 1 und 2 sind auf Darlehen entsprechend anzuwenden, die unmittelbar an Unternehmen zur Verwendung zu den in Absatz 3 bezeichneten Zwecken gegeben worden sind. Für die Ermäßigung der Einkommensteuer oder Körperschaftsteuer ist in diesen Fällen weitere Voraussetzung, daß sich der Darlehnsgeber und der Darlehnsnehmer gegenüber der Berliner Industriebank Aktiengesellschaft oder der Niederlassung Berlin der Industriekreditbank Aktiengesellschaft — Deutsche Industriebank damit einverstanden erklären, daß diese die Verwendung der Darlehen zu den bezeichneten Zwecken und die Durchführung des Darlehnsvertrags überwacht.

(5) Die Ermäßigung der Einkommensteuer oder Körperschaftsteuer nach Absatz 1 darf zusammen mit der Ermäßigung der Einkommensteuer oder Körperschaftsteuer nach § 17 fünfzig vom Hundert der Einkommensteuer oder Körperschaftsteuer nicht übersteigen, die sich ohne die Ermäßigungen ergeben würde.

(6) Die Absätze 1 bis 5 gelten nicht für Kreditinstitute im Sinne des Gesetzes über das Kreditwesen vom 10. Juli 1961 (Bundesgesetzbl. I S. 881)[10].

[10]) GVBl. S. 976, 1084

§ 17

Steuerermäßigung für Darlehen zur Finanzierung von Baumaßnahmen

(1) Bei unbeschränkt Steuerpflichtigen, die unverzinsliche, in gleichen Jahresbeträgen zu tilgende Darlehen mit einer Laufzeit von mindestens zehn Jahren zur Förderung des Baues von Wohnungen in Berlin (West) gewähren, ermäßigt sich unter den Voraussetzungen der Absätze 3 bis 7 die Einkommensteuer oder Körperschaftsteuer für den Veranlagungszeitraum der Hingabe um zwanzig vom Hundert der hingegebenen Darlehen. Werden die Darlehen von Steuerpflichtigen, die den Gewinn nach § 4 Abs. 1 oder § 5 des Einkommensteuergesetzes ermitteln, aus Mitteln des Betriebs gegeben, so sind die Darlehen in der Bilanz mit dem Wert anzusetzen, der sich nach Abzug von Zwischenzinsen unter Berücksichtigung von Zinseszinsen vom Nennbetrag der Darlehen ergibt. Dabei ist von einem Zinssatz von höchstens fünfeinhalb vom Hundert auszugehen. Die Sätze 2 und 3 gelten auch, wenn die Hingabe der Darlehen nicht durch den Betrieb veranlaßt ist. Sind die Darlehen aus Mitteln eines Betriebs gegeben worden, so ermäßigt sich die Einkommensteuer oder Körperschaftsteuer des Veranlagungszeitraums, in dem das Wirtschaftsjahr endet, in dessen Verlauf die Darlehen gegeben worden sind.

(2) Bei unbeschränkt Steuerpflichtigen, die verzinsliche Darlehen mit einer Laufzeit von mindestens 25 Jahren zur Förderung des Baues, des Umbaues, der Erweiterung, der Modernisierung und der Instandsetzung von Gebäuden in Berlin (West) gewähren, ermäßigt sich unter den Voraussetzungen der Absätze 3 bis 7 die Einkommensteuer oder Körperschaftsteuer für den Veranlagungszeitraum der Hingabe um 20 vom Hundert der hingegebenen Darlehen. Satz 1 ist nur anzuwenden, wenn die Darlehen nach den vertraglichen Vereinbarungen

1. höchstens mit gleichen Jahresbeträgen, die der im Darlehnsvertrag vereinbarten Laufzeit entsprechen, zu tilgen oder
2. mit gleichen Jahresbeträgen, bei denen sich bei gleichbleibenden Bedingungen infolge der laufenden Tilgung der Zinsanteil verringert und der Tilgungsanteil entsprechend erhöht, zu verzinsen und zu tilgen sind; Änderungen des Zinssatzes in Anpassung an die allgemeine Zinshöhe sind jedoch zulässig.

Absatz 1 letzter Satz gilt entsprechend.

(3) Voraussetzung für die Steuerermäßigungen nach den Absätzen 1 und 2 ist, daß die Darlehen an einen Bauherrn gegeben werden und von diesem unverzüglich und unmittelbar

1. in den Fällen des Absatzes 1 zur Finanzierung des Baues von Wohnungen im Sinne des § 39 oder § 82 des Zweiten Wohnungsbaugesetzes (Wohnungsbau- und Familienheimgesetz),
2. in den Fällen des Absatzes 2 zur Finanzierung der dort bezeichneten Bauvorhaben

verwendet werden. Für die Anwendung des Absatzes 1 ist weitere Voraussetzung, daß die Darlehen weder unmittelbar noch mittelbar in wirtschaftlichem Zusammenhang mit der Aufnahme eines Kredits stehen. Die Steuerermäßigung nach den Absätzen 1 und 2 wird unter der Bedingung gewährt, daß eine vorzeitige Rückzahlung der Darlehen nicht stattfindet; vorzeitige Rückzahlungen, die nach Ablauf von zehn Jahren seit der Hingabe des Darlehens auf Grund einer Kündigung oder Teilkündigung des Schuldners stattfinden, sind jedoch unschädlich.

(4) Die Vorschriften des Absatzes 1 sind nur anzuwenden, soweit die Darlehen 10 000 Deutsche Mark für jede geförderte Wohnung nicht übersteigen.

(5) Die Vorschriften der Absätze 2 und 3 sind auf Darlehen entsprechend anzuwenden, die der Wohnungsbau-Kreditanstalt Berlin oder der Berliner Pfandbrief-Bank gewährt werden. Die Wohnungsbau-Kreditanstalt Berlin und die Berliner Pfandbrief-Bank haben die Darlehen, gegebenenfalls unter Einschaltung von Berliner Kreditinstituten, an Bauherren weiterzugeben, die die Darlehen unverzüglich und unmittelbar zur Finanzierung der in Absatz 2 bezeichneten Bauvorhaben verwenden. Die Wohnungsbau-Kreditanstalt Berlin und die Berliner Pfandbrief-Bank haben sicherzustellen, daß die Darlehen nur zu diesen Zwecken verwendet werden. Ist der Bedarf an Darlehen für die bezeichneten Zwecke gedeckt, so können die Wohnungsbau-Kreditanstalt Berlin und die Berliner Pfandbrief-Bank den Abschluß weiterer Darlehensverträge ablehnen.

(6) Die Ermäßigung der Einkommensteuer oder Körperschaftsteuer nach den Absätzen 1 und 2 darf zusammen mit der Ermäßigung der Einkommensteuer oder Körperschaftsteuer nach § 16 fünfzig vom Hundert der Einkommensteuer oder Körperschaftsteuer nicht übersteigen, die sich ohne die Ermäßigungen ergeben würde.

(7) Zum Nachweis der in Absatz 1 Satz 1, Absatz 2, Absatz 3 Satz 1 und in den Absätzen 4 und 5 bezeichneten Voraussetzungen ist eine Bescheinigung des Senators für Bau- und Wohnungswesen, Berlin, oder der von ihm bestimmten Stelle vorzulegen.

§ 18

Anwendung der §§ 16 und 17 durch Arbeitnehmer

Besteht das Einkommen ganz oder teilweise aus Einkünften aus nichtselbständiger Arbeit, von denen ein Steuerabzug vorgenommen wird, und liegen die Voraussetzungen des § 46 Abs. 1 und 2 des Einkommensteuergesetzes nicht vor, so kann die Veranlagung zur Anwendung der Vorschriften der §§ 16 und 17 beantragt werden; § 46 Abs. 2 Ziff. 8 Buchstabe a und Abs. 3 und 5 des Einkommensteuergesetzes ist sinngemäß anzuwenden.

Artikel III
Investitionszulage

§ 19

(1) Steuerpflichtige im Sinne des Einkommensteuergesetzes und des Körperschaftsteuergesetzes, die in Berlin (West) einen Betrieb (eine Betriebstätte) haben, können für abnutzbare Wirtschaftsgüter des Anlagevermögens und Ausbauten und Erweiterungen an zum Anlagevermögen gehörenden Gebäuden eine Investitionszulage erhalten. Werden die Wirtschaftsgüter, Ausbauten oder Erweiterungen von einer Gesellschaft im Sinne des § 15 Abs. 1 Ziff. 2 des Einkommensteuergesetzes angeschafft oder hergestellt, gilt Satz 1 mit der Maßgabe, daß der Gesellschaft die Investitionszulage gewährt wird. Die Investitionszulage beträgt 10 vom Hundert der Anschaffungs- oder Herstellungskosten der im Kalenderjahr angeschafften oder hergestellten Wirtschaftsgüter, Ausbauten und Erweiterungen. Sie erhöht sich für abnutzbare bewegliche Wirtschaftsgüter des Anlagevermögens,

1. die in einem Betrieb (einer Betriebstätte)
   a) des verarbeitenden Gewerbes — ausgenommen Baugewerbe — unmittelbar oder mittelbar der Fertigung dienen,
   b) der Energiewirtschaft einschließlich Fernheizwerke unmittelbar oder mittelbar der Erzeugung von Energie oder Wärme dienen,

   auf 25 vom Hundert der Anschaffungs- oder Herstellungskosten;
2. die ausschließlich der Forschung oder Entwicklung im Sinne des § 51 Abs. 1 Ziff. 2 Buchstabe u Satz 4 des Einkommensteuergesetzes dienen, auf 30 vom Hundert der Anschaffungs- oder Herstellungskosten.

Wird der Gewinn nach einem vom Kalenderjahr abweichenden Wirtschaftsjahr ermittelt, so tritt an die Stelle des Kalenderjahrs das Wirtschaftsjahr, das im Kalenderjahr endet.

(2) Die Investitionszulage wird nur für neue abnutzbare bewegliche Wirtschaftsgüter gewährt, die zum Anlagevermögen eines Betriebs (einer Betriebstätte) in Berlin (West) gehören und mindestens drei Jahre nach ihrer Anschaffung oder Herstellung in einem solchen Betrieb (einer solchen Betriebstätte) verbleiben; bei Schiffen tritt an die Stelle des Zeitraums von drei Jahren ein Zeitraum von acht Jahren. Für Personenkraftfahrzeuge wird eine Investitionszulage nur gewährt, wenn sie im eigenen gewerblichen Betrieb ausschließlich der Beförderung von Personen gegen Entgelt dienen oder an Selbstfahrer vermietet oder für Fahrschulzwecke verwendet werden. Für bewegliche Wirtschaftsgüter, deren Anschaffungs- oder Herstellungskosten, vermindert um einen darin enthaltenen Vorsteuerbetrag (§ 9 b Abs. 1 des Einkommensteuergesetzes), 800 Deutsche Mark nicht übersteigen und die einer selbständigen Bewertung und Nutzung fähig sind, wird eine Investitionszulage nicht gewährt. Für Gebäude und für Ausbauten und Erweiterungen an Gebäuden wird die Investitionszulage nur gewährt, wenn die Gebäude, Ausbauten und Erweiterungen in Berlin (West) errichtet werden und die Voraussetzungen des § 14 Abs. 2 Nr. 2 Buchstabe a erfüllen.

(3) Die Investitionszulage kann bereits für im Kalenderjahr (Wirtschaftsjahr) aufgewendete Anzahlungen auf Anschaffungskosten und für Teilher-

stellungskosten von Wirtschaftsgütern, Ausbauten und Erweiterungen im Sinne des Absatzes 2 gewährt werden. Der Gesamtbetrag der Investitionszulage darf auch in diesem Fall die in Absatz 1 bezeichneten Hundertsätze der Anschaffungs- oder Herstellungskosten nicht übersteigen. § 7a Abs. 2 Satz 3 bis 5 des Einkommensteuergesetzes gilt entsprechend.

(4) Die Investitionszulage wird auf Antrag nach Ablauf des Kalenderjahrs, in dem die Wirtschaftsgüter, Ausbauten und Erweiterungen angezahlt, angeschafft oder ganz oder teilweise hergestellt worden sind (bei einem vom Kalenderjahr abweichenden Wirtschaftsjahr: nach Ablauf des Kalenderjahrs, in dem das Wirtschaftsjahr endet, in dem die Wirtschaftsgüter, Ausbauten und Erweiterungen angezahlt, angeschafft oder ganz oder teilweise hergestellt worden sind), durch das für den Antragsteller für die Besteuerung nach dem Einkommen zuständige Finanzamt aus den Einnahmen an Einkommensteuer oder Körperschaftsteuer gewährt. Personengesellschaften wird die Investitionszulage von dem Finanzamt gewährt, das für die einheitliche und gesonderte Feststellung der Einkünfte zuständig ist. Der Antrag auf Gewährung der Investitionszulage kann nur innerhalb von drei Monaten nach Ablauf des Kalenderjahrs gestellt werden.

(5) Das Finanzamt setzt die Investitionszulage durch schriftlichen Bescheid fest. Die Investitionszulage ist innerhalb eines Monats nach Bekanntgabe des Bescheids fällig.

(6) Wird nach der Auszahlung der Investitionszulage festgestellt, daß die Voraussetzungen für ihre Gewährung nicht oder nur zum Teil vorgelegen haben, so ist die Investitionszulage insoweit zurückzuzahlen, als sie zu Unrecht gewährt worden ist. Das gleiche gilt, wenn Wirtschaftsgüter, deren Anschaffungs- oder Herstellungkosten bei der Bemessung der Investitionszulage berücksichtigt worden sind, nicht mindestens drei Jahre (bei Schiffen nicht mindestens acht Jahre) seit ihrer Anschaffung oder Herstellung in einem Betrieb (einer Betriebstätte) in Berlin (West) verblieben sind. Das Finanzamt fordert den Betrag durch schriftlichen Bescheid zurück. Der Anspruch auf Rückzahlung der Investitionszulage entsteht,

1. wenn die Voraussetzungen für ihre Gewährung nicht oder nur zum Teil vorgelegen haben,
   mit der Auszahlung der Investitionszulage;
2. wenn die bei ihrer Bemessung berücksichtigten Wirtschaftsgüter nicht mindestens drei Jahre (bei Schiffen nicht mindestens acht Jahre) seit ihrer Anschaffung oder Herstellung in einem Betrieb (einer Betriebstätte) in Berlin (West) verblieben sind,
   mit dem Ausscheiden der Wirtschaftsgüter aus dem Betrieb (der Betriebstätte) in Berlin (West).

Der Anspruch auf Rückzahlung ist vom Zeitpunkt seiner Entstehung an nach § 5 des Steuersäumnisgesetzes zu verzinsen.

(7) Die Investitionszulage gehört nicht zu den Einkünften im Sinne des Einkommensteuergesetzes. Sie mindert nicht die steuerlichen Anschaffungs- oder Herstellungskosten.

(8) Die Vorschriften des Ersten und Zweiten Teils der Reichsabgabenordnung, des Steueranpassungsgesetzes und des Steuersäumnisgesetzes sind entsprechend anzuwenden. Der Anspruch auf Rückzahlung der Investitionszulage verjährt in fünf Jahren. Gegen die Bescheide nach den Absätzen 5 und 6 ist der Einspruch gegeben.

(9) In öffentlich-rechtlichen Streitigkeiten über die auf Grund dieses Artikels ergehenden Verwaltungsakte der Finanzbehörden ist der Finanzrechtsweg gegeben.

§ 20

(gestrichen)

Abschnitt II

Steuererleichterungen und Arbeitnehmervergünstigungen

Artikel IV

Einkommensteuer (Lohnsteuer) und Körperschaftsteuer

§ 21

Ermäßigung der veranlagten Einkommensteuer und Körperschaftsteuer

(1) Bei zur Einkommensteuer veranlagten Personen, die

1. ihren ausschließlichen Wohnsitz in Berlin (West) zu Beginn des Veranlagungszeitraums haben oder ihn im Laufe des Veranlagungszeitraums begründen oder
2. bei mehrfachem Wohnsitz während des ganzen Veranlagungszeitraums einen Wohnsitz in Berlin (West) haben und dort veranlagt werden oder
3. — ohne einen Wohnsitz im Geltungsbereich dieses Gesetzes zu haben — ihren gewöhnlichen Aufenthalt in Berlin (West) haben,

ermäßigt sich die tarifliche Einkommensteuer (§ 32a Abs. 1 und 5 des Einkommensteuergesetzes), soweit sie auf Einkünfte aus Berlin (West) im Sinne des § 23 entfällt, um 30 vom Hundert. Bei Ehegatten im Sinne des § 26 Abs. 1 des Einkommensteuergesetzes genügt es für die Ermäßigung, wenn einer der Ehegatten die Voraussetzungen des Satzes 1 erfüllt. Die Ermäßigung der Einkommensteuer, die auf Einkünfte aus nichtselbständiger Arbeit im Sinne des § 23 Nr. 4 Buchstabe a entfällt, ist durch die für den Veranlagungszeitraum gezahlten Zulagen nach § 28 Abs. 1 Satz 1 abgegolten, soweit sie diese nicht übersteigt. Zulagen zum Arbeitslohn, von dem die Lohnsteuer nach § 40a des Einkommensteuergesetzes mit einem Pauschsteuersatz erhoben worden ist, bleiben außer Betracht.

(2) Bei Körperschaften, Personenvereinigungen und Vermögensmassen, die ihre Geschäftsleitung und ihren Sitz ausschließlich in Berlin (West)

haben, ermäßigt sich die tarifliche Körperschaftsteuer (§§ 19 und 19a Abs. 6 des Körperschaftsteuergesetzes), soweit sie auf Einkünfte aus Berlin (West) im Sinne des § 23 entfällt, um 20 vom Hundert und um 3,2 vom Hundert der in dem Einkommen enthaltenen Einkünfte aus Berlin (West) im Sinne des § 23.

(3) Bei Steuerpflichtigen, die, ohne die Voraussetzungen der Absätze 1 und 2 zu erfüllen, eine oder mehrere Betriebstätten eines Gewerbebetriebs in Berlin (West) unterhalten, in denen während des Veranlagungszeitraums im Durchschnitt regelmäßig insgesamt mindestens 25 Arbeitnehmer beschäftigt worden sind, ermäßigt sich die tarifliche Einkommensteuer um 30 vom Hundert oder die tarifliche Körperschaftsteuer um 20 vom Hundert, soweit sie nach § 23 Nr. 2 auf Einkünfte aus diesen Betriebstätten entfällt; die tarifliche Körperschaftsteuer ermäßigt sich außerdem um 3,2 vom Hundert dieser in dem Einkommen enthaltenen Einkünfte aus Berlin (West) im Sinne des § 23 Nr. 2. Ist der Steuerpflichtige Mitunternehmer im Sinne des § 15 Abs. 1 Ziff. 2 des Einkommensteuergesetzes, so genügt es, wenn die in Satz 1 bezeichnete Mindestzahl von Arbeitnehmern insgesamt in den in Berlin (West) unterhaltenen Betriebstätten des Unternehmens, an dem der Steuerpflichtige beteiligt ist, beschäftigt worden ist. Unterhält ein Steuerpflichtiger Betriebstätten mehrerer Gewerbebetriebe in Berlin (West), so wird die Ermäßigung nur insoweit gewährt, als in den Betriebstätten des einzelnen Gewerbebetriebs die in Satz 1 bezeichnete Mindestzahl von Arbeitnehmern beschäftigt worden ist.

§ 22

Ermäßigung der veranlagten Einkommensteuer bei Zuzug von Arbeitnehmern

Bei zur Einkommensteuer veranlagten Arbeitnehmern, die, ohne die Voraussetzungen des § 21 Abs. 1 zu erfüllen, in Berlin (West) ihren Aufenthalt begründen und dort eine nichtselbständige Beschäftigung für einen zusammenhängenden Zeitraum von mindestens drei Monaten aufnehmen, ermäßigt sich die tarifliche Einkommensteuer (§ 32 a Abs. 1 und 5 des Einkommensteuergesetzes), soweit sie auf Einkünfte im Sinne des § 23 Nr. 4 Buchstabe a aus dieser Beschäftigung entfällt, um 30 vom Hundert. § 21 Abs. 1 Satz 3 und 4 gilt entsprechend.

§ 23

Einkünfte aus Berlin (West)

Einkünfte aus Berlin (West) im Sinne des § 21 sind

1. Einkünfte aus in Berlin (West) betriebener Land- und Forstwirtschaft;
2. Einkünfte aus Gewerbebetrieb, die in einer Betriebstätte in Berlin (West) erzielt worden sind. Hat ein Gewerbebetrieb Betriebstätten (Teile von Betriebstätten) in Berlin (West) und an anderen Orten unterhalten, so gilt als Gewinn der Betriebstätten in Berlin (West) der Teil des Gesamtgewinns, der sich aus dem Verhältnis ergibt, in dem die Arbeitslöhne, die an die bei den Betriebstätten in Berlin (West) beschäftigten Arbeitnehmer gezahlt worden sind, zu der Summe der Arbeitslöhne stehen, die an die bei allen Betriebstätten beschäftigten Arbeitnehmer gezahlt worden sind. Für den Begriff der Arbeitslöhne sind die Vorschriften des § 31 des Gewerbesteuergesetzes maßgebend. Liegen Veräußerungsgewinne im Sinne des § 16 des Einkommensteuergesetzes vor, so tritt insoweit an die Stelle der Aufteilung nach dem Verhältnis der Arbeitslöhne eine Aufteilung nach dem Verhältnis der Werte des anteiligen Betriebsvermögens, die für die Berechnung des Veräußerungsgewinns zugrunde gelegt werden;
3. Einkünfte aus selbständiger Arbeit, soweit sie aus einer in Berlin (West) ausgeübten Tätigkeit erzielt worden sind;
4. Einkünfte aus nichtselbständiger Arbeit, wenn der Arbeitslohn
   a) für eine Beschäftigung in Berlin (West) aus einem gegenwärtigen Dienstverhältnis bezogen wird. Wird im Rahmen einer solchen Beschäftigung Arbeitslohn für eine vorübergehende Tätigkeit außerhalb von Berlin (West) bezogen, so liegen Einkünfte in diesem Sinne dann vor, wenn die Arbeitnehmer ihren ausschließlichen Wohnsitz in Berlin (West) haben. Bei Ehegatten, die beide unbeschränkt steuerpflichtig sind und nicht dauernd getrennt leben, genügt es, wenn einer der Ehegatten seinen ausschließlichen Wohnsitz in Berlin (West) hat. Eine vorübergehende Tätigkeit außerhalb von Berlin (West) ist jeweils höchstens für die Dauer von zwölf Monaten anzunehmen, wenn sich die Arbeitnehmer anläßlich einer Dienstreise oder einer Tätigkeit, die auf eine bestimmte Zeit oder auf die Zeit der Durchführung eines bestimmten Vorhabens begrenzt ist, außerhalb von Berlin (West) aufhalten. Zum Arbeitslohn aus einem gegenwärtigen Dienstverhältnis im Sinne dieser Vorschrift gehören auch Bezüge und Vorteile aus früheren Dienstleistungen, die gleichzeitig mit anderem Arbeitslohn aus einem gegenwärtigen Dienstverhältnis von demselben Arbeitgeber oder aus derselben öffentlichen Kasse bezogen werden,
   b) vorbehaltlich der Regelung in Buchstabe a letzter Satz als Wartegeld, Ruhegeld, Witwen- und Waisengeld oder andere Bezüge und Vorteile aus früheren Dienstleistungen zufließt;
5. Einkünfte aus Kapitalvermögen
   a) im Sinne des § 20 Abs. 1 Ziff. 1, 2, 4, 5 und 6 des Einkommensteuergesetzes, wenn der Steuerpflichtige nachweist,
      aa) daß der Schuldner der Kapitalerträge seinen ausschließlichen Wohnsitz oder seine Geschäftsleitung und seinen Sitz in Berlin (West) hat oder
      bb) daß es sich um Zinsen auf Einlagen einschließlich Darlehen bei einer in Berlin (West) belegenen Betriebstätte eines Kreditinstituts handelt,

b) im Sinne des § 20 Abs. 1 Ziff. 3 des Einkommensteuergesetzes, wenn das Kapitalvermögen durch Grundbesitz in Berlin (West), durch Rechte in Berlin (West), die den Vorschriften des bürgerlichen Rechts über Grundstücke unterliegen, oder durch Schiffe, die in ein Schiffsregister in Berlin (West) eingetragen sind, gesichert ist;

6. Einkünfte aus Vermietung und Verpachtung im Sinne des § 21 Abs. 1 und 2 des Einkommensteuergesetzes, wenn das unbewegliche Vermögen, die Sachinbegriffe, gewerblichen Erfahrungen oder Gerechtigkeiten in Berlin (West) belegen oder in ein öffentliches Buch oder Register in Berlin (West) eingetragen sind oder in einer in Berlin (West) belegenen Betriebstätte verwertet werden;

7. Einkünfte im Sinne des § 22 des Einkommensteuergesetzes.

§ 24

Behandlung von Organgesellschaften und verbundenen Unternehmen

(1) In den Fällen des § 7 a des Körperschaftsteuergesetzes sind für die Ermittlung der in Betriebstätten in Berlin (West) erzielten Einkünfte aus Gewerbebetrieb (§ 23 Nr. 2) Organgesellschaften als Betriebstätten des Organträgers anzusehen.

(2) Bestehen bei einem Unternehmen mit einem oder mehreren anderen Unternehmen, ohne daß die Voraussetzungen des Absatzes 1 vorliegen, Verbindungen organisatorischer, finanzieller oder wirtschaftlicher Art, so kann das Finanzamt für die Zwecke der Ermäßigung der Einkommensteuer oder Körperschaftsteuer den Gewinn aus Gewerbebetrieb dieses Unternehmens abweichend von dem bei der Veranlagung zugrunde gelegten Gewinn ansetzen. Maßgebend ist der Gewinn, der sich nach den Verhältnissen des Unternehmens ohne die bezeichneten Verbindungen ergeben hätte.

§ 25

Berechnung der Ermäßigung der veranlagten Einkommensteuer und Körperschaftsteuer

(1) Sind in dem Einkommen nur Einkünfte aus Berlin (West) enthalten oder beträgt der Gesamtbetrag der Einkünfte nicht mehr als 3 000 Deutsche Mark, so wird die Ermäßigung vorbehaltlich des Absatzes 3 in vollem Umfang gewährt.

(2) Sind in dem Einkommen neben den Einkünften aus Berlin (West) noch andere Einkünfte enthalten, so ist die Einkommensteuer oder Körperschaftsteuer für die Berechnung der Ermäßigung

1. bei Steuerpflichtigen im Sinne des § 21 Abs. 1 und 2 im Verhältnis der Summe aller Einkünfte aus Berlin (West) — § 23 — zum Gesamtbetrag der Einkünfte,

2. bei Steuerpflichtigen im Sinne des § 22 im Verhältnis der nach dieser Vorschrift für die Ermäßigung zu berücksichtigenden Einkünfte aus nichtselbständiger Arbeit aus Berlin (West) zum Gesamtbetrag der Einkünfte,

3. bei Steuerpflichtigen im Sinne des § 21 Abs. 3 im Verhältnis der für die Ermäßigung zu berücksichtigenden Einkünfte aus Gewerbebetrieb aus Berlin (West) — § 23 Nr. 2 — zum Gesamtbetrag der Einkünfte

aufzuteilen. Beträgt die Summe der für die Ermäßigung der Einkommensteuer oder Körperschaftsteuer nicht zu berücksichtigenden Einkünfte nicht mehr als 3 000 Deutsche Mark, so wird die Ermäßigung vorbehaltlich des Absatzes 3 in vollem Umfang gewährt.

(3) Bestehen die Einkünfte aus Berlin (West) ausschließlich aus Einkünften aus nichtselbständiger Arbeit im Sinne des § 23 Nr. 4 Buchstabe a, so wird die nach den Absätzen 1 und 2 berechnete Ermäßigung nur insoweit gewährt, als sie die Zulagen nach § 28 Abs. 1 Satz 1 und 2 übersteigt. Bestehen die Einkünfte aus Berlin (West) nur zum Teil aus Einkünften aus nichtselbständiger Arbeit im Sinne des § 23 Nr. 4 Buchstabe a, so ist die Ermäßigung im Verhältnis der letztgenannten Einkünfte in den Fällen des Absatzes 1 und des Absatzes 2 Satz 2 zum Gesamtbetrag der Einkünfte und in den Fällen des Absatzes 2 Satz 1 zur Summe der Einkünfte aus Berlin (West) aufzuteilen. Die Ermäßigung, die hiernach auf die Einkünfte aus nichtselbständiger Arbeit im Sinne des § 23 Nr. 4 Buchstabe a entfällt, wird nur insoweit gewährt, als sie die Zulagen nach § 28 Abs. 1 Satz 1 und 2 übersteigt.

(4) Durch Rechtsverordnung kann bestimmt werden, daß Einkünfte, bei denen die Einkommensteuer oder Körperschaftsteuer durch den Steuerabzug als abgegolten gilt, im Fall des Absatzes 2 unberücksichtigt bleiben, Freibeträge, Verlustabzüge, nicht entnommene Gewinne, abzuziehende ausländische Einkommensteuer oder Körperschaftsteuer von den Einkünften abgezogen werden, mit denen sie wirtschaftlich zusammenhängen oder auf die sie sich beziehen, nachzuversteuernde Mehrentnahmen diesen hinzugerechnet werden. Desgleichen kann durch Rechtsverordnung bestimmt werden, daß in den Fällen der §§ 34 und 34 b des Einkommensteuergesetzes die außerordentlichen Einkünfte und die darauf entfallende Einkommensteuer von der Aufteilung nach Absatz 2 ausgenommen oder für die Berechnung der Ermäßigung nach den Grundsätzen des Absatzes 2 gesondert berücksichtigt werden.

§ 26

Ermäßigung der Lohnsteuer

(1) Die Lohnsteuer, die auf Einkünfte aus Berlin (West) im Sinne des § 23 Nr. 4 Buchstabe b entfällt, ermäßigt sich um 30 vom Hundert bei Arbeitnehmern, die

a) ihren ausschließlichen Wohnsitz in Berlin (West) zu Beginn des Kalenderjahres haben oder ihn im Laufe des Kalenderjahres begründen oder

b) bei mehrfachem Wohnsitz während des ganzen Kalenderjahres einen Wohnsitz in Berlin (West) haben und sich dort überwiegend aufhalten oder

c) — ohne einen Wohnsitz im Geltungsbereich dieses Gesetzes zu haben — ihren gewöhnlichen Aufenthalt in Berlin (West) haben.

Bei Ehegatten, die beide unbeschränkt steuerpflichtig sind und nicht dauernd getrennt leben, genügt es für die Ermäßigung, wenn einer der Ehegatten die Voraussetzungen erfüllt.

(2) Wird für die in Absatz 1 genannten Arbeitnehmer ein Lohnsteuer-Jahresausgleich durchgeführt, so ist die nach den § 42 Abs. 4, § 42 a Abs. 2 oder § 42 b Abs. 2 des Einkommensteuergesetzes ermittelte Jahreslohnsteuer für die Berechnung des Erstattungsbetrags um 30 vom Hundert zu ermäßigen, soweit sie auf Einkünfte im Sinne des § 23 Nr. 4 Buchstabe b entfällt.

(3) Beziehen Arbeitnehmer neben Einkünften aus Berlin (West) im Sinne des § 23 Nr. 4 Buchstabe b andere Einkünfte aus nichtselbständiger Arbeit, so gelten für die Berechnung der Ermäßigung die Vorschriften des § 25 Abs. 2 entsprechend.

§ 27

(gestrichen)

Artikel V
Vergünstigung für Arbeitnehmer in Berlin (West)

§ 28

Vergünstigung durch Zulagen

(1) Arbeitnehmer, die Arbeitslohn für eine Beschäftigung in Berlin (West) aus einem gegenwärtigen Dienstverhältnis beziehen (§ 23 Nr. 4 Buchstabe a), erhalten unbeschadet der Steuererleichterungen nach den Vorschriften der §§ 21, 22 und 26 eine Vergünstigung durch Gewährung von Zulagen. Das gilt auch, solange bei Unterbrechung oder Einschränkung der Beschäftigung im Rahmen eines solchen Dienstverhältnisses der Arbeitslohn fortgezahlt wird. Wird bei einer Unterbrechung oder Einschränkung der Beschäftigung der Arbeitslohn nicht oder nicht mehr fortgezahlt, so werden Zulagen je Kalendertag weitergewährt, solange

1. der Arbeitnehmer nachweislich erkrankt ist oder
2. Krankengeld aus der gesetzlichen Krankenversicherung,
3. Verletztengeld aus der gesetzlichen Unfallversicherung,
4. Einkommensausgleich nach § 17 des Bundesversorgungsgesetzes,
5. Kurzarbeitergeld oder Schlechtwettergeld,
6. Mutterschaftsgeld nach den Vorschriften des Mutterschutzgesetzes oder der Reichsversicherungsordnung,
7. Übergangsgeld während der Durchführung von Maßnahmen zur Erhaltung, Besserung und Wiederherstellung der Erwerbsfähigkeit (Heilbehandlung und Berufsförderung),
8. Unterhaltsgeld während der Teilnahme an Maßnahmen der beruflichen Bildung oder der beruflichen Rehabilitation nach dem Arbeitsförderungsgesetz,
9. Unterhaltsbeitrag während einer Berufsförderungsmaßnahme nach § 26 des Bundesversorgungsgesetzes,
10. Entschädigung nach dem Bundesseuchengesetz

bezogen wird, höchstens aber für die Dauer von 78 Wochen. Die Zulage wird auch Arbeitnehmern gewährt, die Konkursausfallgeld nach dem Arbeitsförderungsgesetz beziehen; dabei sind die Zeiten zu berücksichtigen, für die der Arbeitnehmer noch Ansprüche auf Arbeitsentgelt hat, die seinen Anspruch auf Konkursausfallgeld begründen. Das gilt nicht, soweit für diese Zeiten bereits Zulagen gewährt worden sind. Die Zulagen gelten weder als steuerpflichtige Einnahmen im Sinne des Einkommensteuergesetzes noch als Einkommen, Verdienst oder Entgelt im Sinne der Sozialversicherung, der Arbeitslosenversicherung und der Arbeitslosenhilfe. Sie gelten arbeitsrechtlich nicht als Bestandteil des Lohns oder Gehalts.

(2) Bemessungsgrundlage für die Zulage nach Absatz 1 Satz 1 und 2 ist der aus einem gegenwärtigen Dienstverhältnis bezogene Arbeitslohn (§ 23 Nr. 4 Buchstabe a) des Lohnabrechnungszeitraums. In den Fällen des Absatzes 1 Satz 3 ist Bemessungsgrundlage für die Zulage der auf einen Kalendertag entfallende Arbeitslohn des Lohnabrechnungszeitraums. Maßgebend ist der der Unterbrechung oder Einschränkung vorhergehende Lohnabrechnungszeitraum; hat das Dienstverhältnis erst im laufenden Lohnabrechnungszeitraum begonnen, so ist Bemessungsgrundlage für die Zulage der auf einen Kalendertag umgerechnete Arbeitslohn, der bei der für den Arbeitnehmer maßgebenden regelmäßigen Arbeitszeit für den Lohnabrechnungszeitraum ohne die Unterbrechung oder Einschränkung zu zahlen wäre. Arbeitslohn des Lohnabrechnungszeitraums sind der laufende Arbeitslohn, der für den Lohnabrechnungszeitraum gezahlt wird, und sonstige Bezüge, die in dem Lohnabrechnungszeitraum zufließen. Bezüge, von denen die Lohnsteuer nach § 40 und § 40b des Einkommensteuergesetzes mit einem Pauschsteuersatz erhoben wird, und steuerfreie Einnahmen mit Ausnahme der steuerfreien Zuschläge für Sonntags-, Feiertags- und Nachtarbeit (§ 3 b des Einkommensteuergesetzes) bleiben außer Betracht.

(3) Bemessungsgrundlage für die Zulage nach Absatz 1 Satz 4 ist das Arbeitsentgelt aus einer Beschäftigung in Berlin (West) (§ 23 Nr. 4 Buchstabe a), das den Anspruch auf Konkursausfallgeld begründet (§§ 141 b, 141 c des Arbeitsförderungsgesetzes). Absatz 2 Satz 5 ist sinngemäß anzuwenden.

(4) Die Bemessungsgrundlage für die Zulage nach Absatz 1 Satz 1 und 2 ist bei monatlicher Lohnabrechnung auf einen durch 10, bei wöchentlicher Lohnabrechnung auf einen durch 2,5 und bei täglicher Lohnabrechnung auf einen durch 0,5 ohne Rest teilbaren Betrag aufzurunden; bei anderen Lohnabrechnungszeiträumen ergibt sich die Bemessungsgrundlage aus dem mit der Zahl der Arbeitstage vervielfachten Tagesarbeitslohn, der auf einen durch 0,5 ohne Rest teilbaren Betrag aufzurunden ist. Zur Feststellung der Zahl der Arbeitstage sind von der Zahl der Kalendertage des Lohnabrechnungszeitraums für je 7 Tage 2 Tage abzuziehen.

Die Bemessungsgrundlage für die Zulage nach Absatz 1 Satz 3 ist auf einen durch 0,5 ohne Rest teilbaren Betrag und für die Zulage nach Absatz 1 Satz 4 auf einen durch 10 ohne Rest teilbaren Betrag aufzurunden.

(5) Die Zulage beträgt 8 vom Hundert der Bemessungsgrundlage zuzüglich eines Zuschlags für jedes Kind des Arbeitnehmers, das auf seiner Lohnsteuerkarte oder auf einer entsprechenden Bescheinigung für den jeweiligen Lohnabrechnungszeitraum eingetragen ist. Bei Arbeitnehmern, bei denen der Lohnsteuerabzug nach den Steuerklassen II und III vorgenommen wird, beträgt der Kinderzuschlag 22 Deutsche Mark monatlich, 5 Deutsche Mark wöchentlich oder eine Deutsche Mark täglich für jedes Kind. Bei anderen als den in Absatz 4 erster Halbsatz genannten Lohnabrechnungszeiträumen beträgt der Zuschlag eine Deutsche Mark je Arbeitstag (Absatz 4 Satz 2). Wird der Steuerabzug nach der Steuerklasse IV durchgeführt, ermäßigen sich die in den Sätzen 2 und 3 genannten Beträge des Kinderzuschlags um 50 vom Hundert.

(6) Der Arbeitgeber hat die Zulagen zu errechnen. Er hat sie

1. bei monatlichen oder längeren Lohnabrechnungszeiträumen jeweils zusammen mit dem Arbeitslohn,
2. bei kürzeren als monatlichen Lohnabrechnungszeiträumen jeweils für alle in einem Kalendermonat endenden Lohnabrechnungszeiträume zusammen mit dem Arbeitslohn für den letzten in dem Kalendermonat endenden Lohnabrechnungszeitraum

auszuzahlen. In den den Arbeitnehmern erteilten Lohnabrechnungen sind der Arbeitslohn und die Zulagen getrennt auszuweisen. Der Arbeitgeber hat die Summe der Zulagen dem Betrag, den er für seine Arbeitnehmer insgesamt an Lohnsteuer einbehalten hat, zu entnehmen und bei der nächsten Lohnsteueranmeldung in einer Summe abzusetzen. Übersteigt der zu entnehmende Betrag den Betrag, der insgesamt an Lohnsteuer einbehalten ist, so wird der übersteigende Betrag dem Arbeitgeber auf Antrag von dem Finanzamt, an das die Lohnsteuer abzuführen wäre, aus den Einnahmen an Lohnsteuer ersetzt. Die vom Arbeitgeber entnommenen Beträge (Satz 4), die vom Finanzamt ersetzten Beträge (Satz 5) sowie etwa vom Finanzamt selbst ausgezahlte Zulagen mindern die Lohnsteuereinnahmen.

(7) Die Zulage nach Absatz 1 Satz 4 ist von dem zuständigen Arbeitsamt zu errechnen und zusammen mit dem Konkursausfallgeld auszuzahlen; sie ist den Arbeitnehmern gegenüber gesondert auszuweisen. Die ausgezahlten Zulagen werden dem Arbeitsamt auf Antrag von dem Finanzamt, an das der Arbeitgeber die Lohnsteuer abzuführen hätte, aus den Einnahmen an Lohnsteuer ersetzt. Absatz 6 letzter Satz gilt entsprechend.

(8) Hat das Arbeitsamt den Konkursverwalter mit der Errechnung und Auszahlung des Konkursausfallgeldes beauftragt (§ 141 i des Arbeitsförderungsgesetzes), so hat der Konkursverwalter auch die Zulage zu errechnen und auszuzahlen. Die Mittel für die Auszahlung werden vom Arbeitsamt dem Konkursverwalter zur Verfügung gestellt und dem Arbeitsamt auf Antrag von dem Finanzamt, an das der Arbeitgeber die Lohnsteuer abzuführen hätte, ersetzt.

(9) Soweit die in Absatz 1 Satz 3 bezeichneten Leistungen nicht vom Arbeitgeber ausgezahlt werden, hat der Arbeitnehmer die Voraussetzungen für einen Zulagenanspruch nach Absatz 1 Satz 3 gegenüber dem Arbeitgeber nachzuweisen. Der Nachweis ist durch Vorlage von Belegen über den Bezug einer der in Absatz 1 Satz 3 bezeichneten Leistungen zu erbringen. Der Arbeitgeber hat die Art der Leistung und den Zeitraum, für den sie gezahlt worden ist, im Lohnkonto zu vermerken.

(10) Der Anspruch auf die Zulage ist nicht übertragbar.

§ 29

Ergänzende Vorschriften

(1) Die Vorschriften des Ersten und Zweiten Teils der Reichsabgabenordnung und des Steueranpassungsgesetzes sind entsprechend anzuwenden, soweit in den folgenden Absätzen nicht etwas anderes vorgeschrieben ist.

(2) Der Arbeitnehmer kann beantragen, daß das Finanzamt, an das der Arbeitgeber die Lohnsteuer abzuführen hat oder in den Fällen des § 28 Abs. 7 und 8 abzuführen hätte, die Zulage durch schriftlichen Bescheid festsetzt. Der Antrag ist bis zum Ablauf von zwei Monaten nach dem Ende des Zeitraums, für den die Zulage nach § 28 Abs. 6 Satz 2 auszuzahlen ist, in den Fällen des § 28 Abs. 7 und 8 bis zum Ablauf von zwei Monaten nach der Auszahlung des Konkursausfallgeldes, zu stellen. Die Frist kann auf Antrag verlängert werden. Das Finanzamt fordert zu Unrecht ausgezahlte Zulagen durch schriftlichen Bescheid zurück, wenn es feststellt, daß die Voraussetzungen für die Gewährung der Zulagen nicht vorgelegen haben. Der Rückforderungsanspruch entsteht mit der Auszahlung der Zulage. Er verjährt in fünf Jahren. Gegen die Bescheide nach den Sätzen 1 und 3 ist der Einspruch gegeben.

(3) Ist eine Zulage durch Bescheid rechtskräftig festgesetzt worden, so ist der Arbeitgeber verpflichtet, die Zulage an den Arbeitnehmer nach Maßgabe des rechtskräftigen Bescheids zu zahlen, wenn nicht das Finanzamt die Zulage selbst auszahlt. Das Finanzamt hat dem Arbeitgeber eine Abschrift des rechtskräftigen Bescheids zu übersenden.

(4) Der Arbeitgeber haftet für zu Unrecht gezahlte Zulagen. Das Finanzamt hat auf Anfrage des Arbeitgebers oder in den Fällen des § 28 Abs. 1 Satz 4 auf Anfrage des Arbeitsamts oder des Konkursverwalters Auskunft über die Anwendung der Vorschriften über die Gewährung der Zulagen im einzelnen Fall zu erteilen.

(5) Der Arbeitgeber hat die nach § 28 Abs. 1 Satz 1 bis 3 gezahlten Zulagen bei jeder Lohnabrechnung im Lohnkonto des Arbeitnehmers oder, sofern ein Lohnkonto nicht zu führen ist, in entsprechenden Aufzeichnungen voneinander getrennt einzutragen.

In der Lohnsteuerbescheinigung und im Lohnzettel sind nur die Zulagen nach § 28 Abs. 1 Satz 1 und 2 besonders zu bescheinigen.

(6) Beträge, die beim Finanzamt auf Grund eines mit der Zahlung der Zulagen zusammenhängenden Tatbestandes, insbesondere auf Grund einer Rückforderung von Zulagen vom Arbeitnehmer oder einer Inanspruchnahme des Arbeitgebers im Rahmen seiner Haftung, eingehen, erhöhen die Lohnsteuereinnahmen.

(7) In öffentlich-rechtlichen Streitigkeiten über die auf Grund dieses Artikels ergehenden Verwaltungsakte der Finanzbehörden ist der Finanzrechtsweg gegeben.

Artikel VI
Ermächtigungsvorschriften

§ 30

(1) Die Bundesregierung wird ermächtigt, mit Zustimmung des Bundesrates

1. zur Durchführung dieses Abschnitts Rechtsverordnungen zu erlassen, soweit dies zur Wahrung der Gleichmäßigkeit bei der Besteuerung und bei der Gewährung der Zulagen, zur Beseitigung von Unbilligkeiten in Härtefällen oder zur Verwaltungsvereinfachung erforderlich ist, und zwar
   a) über die Abgrenzung des begünstigten Personenkreises,
   b) über die Ermittlung und Abgrenzung der Einkünfte aus Berlin (West) einschließlich der darauf entfallenden Betriebsausgaben und Werbungskosten;
2. Vorschriften durch Rechtsverordnung zu erlassen
   a) über das Verfahren bei der Gewährung von Zulagen,
   b) über die Ersetzung von Zulagen an Arbeitgeber, wenn die Summe der Zulagen den Betrag übersteigt, der insgesamt an Lohnsteuer einbehalten ist; dabei kann auch eine Verrechnung mit anderen Abgaben oder Beiträgen des Arbeitgebers zugelassen werden. Die verrechneten Beträge sind vom Finanzamt wie Minderungen der Lohnsteuereinnahmen zu behandeln;
3. die in § 25 Abs. 4 vorgesehenen Rechtsverordnungen zu erlassen.

(2) Der Bundesminister der Finanzen wird ermächtigt, zur Berechnung der nach den §§ 21, 22 und 26 zu ermäßigenden Einkommensteuer und Lohnsteuer aus der Einkommensteuertabelle und der Jahreslohnsteuertabelle abgeleitete Tabellen aufzustellen und bekanntzumachen. Bei der Aufstellung der abgeleiteten Tabellen sind die gleichen Abrundungen vorzunehmen wie bei der Aufstellung der Ausgangstabellen. Für die Aufstellung und Bekanntmachung von Lohnsteuertabellen für monatliche, wöchentliche und tägliche Lohnzahlungen sind die für die allgemeinen Lohnsteuertabellen maßgebenden Vorschriften anzuwenden.

(3) Der Bundesminister der Finanzen wird ermächtigt, zur Berechnung der Zulagen nach § 28 bei monatlicher, wöchentlicher und täglicher Lohnabrechnung Tabellen aufzustellen und bekanntzumachen.

Abschnitt III
Schlußvorschriften

§ 31
Anwendungsbereich

(1) Die vorstehende Fassung dieses Gesetzes ist, soweit in den folgenden Absätzen nichts anderes bestimmt ist, erstmals für den Veranlagungszeitraum 1975 anzuwenden. Beim Steuerabzug vom Arbeitslohn gilt Satz 1 mit der Maßgabe, daß die vorstehende Fassung dieses Gesetzes erstmals auf den laufenden Arbeitslohn, der für einen nach dem 31. Dezember 1974 endenden Lohnzahlungszeitraum gezahlt wird, und auf sonstige Bezüge, die nach dem 31. Dezember 1974 zufließen, anzuwenden ist. Für die Gewährung von Zulagen nach § 28 gilt Satz 1 mit der Maßgabe, daß die vorstehende Fassung dieses Gesetzes erstmals auf Lohnabrechnungszeiträume anzuwenden ist, die nach dem 31. Dezember 1974 enden. Überschreitet der Lohnabrechnungszeitraum 5 Wochen, so tritt an seine Stelle der Lohnzahlungszeitraum.

(2) Die Vorschriften der §§ 1 bis 13 sind vorbehaltlich der Absätze 3 bis 5 auf Umsätze und Innenumsätze anzuwenden, die nach dem 31. Dezember 1975 ausgeführt werden.

(3) Abweichend von Absatz 2 sind die Vorschriften des § 4 Abs. 1 Nr. 10 in der Fassung des Gesetzes zur Änderung des Berlinförderungsgesetzes und anderer Gesetze vom 19. Dezember 1975 (Bundesgesetzbl. I S. 3157), des § 4 Abs. 1 Nr. 15 und Abs. 3 Nr. 5 und 6 auf Umsätze und Innenumsätze anzuwenden, die nach dem 31. Dezember 1977 ausgeführt werden.

(4) Bei Schrott, Alt- und Abfallmaterial einschließlich Bearbeitungsabfälle ist das Entgelt oder Verrechnungsentgelt für die Kürzungen nach § 1 Abs. 1, § 1 a Abs. 1 und § 2 Abs. 1 zu mindern,

a) bei Umsätzen und Innenumsätzen, die nach dem 31. Dezember 1975 und vor dem 1. Januar 1977 ausgeführt werden, um 25 vom Hundert,

b) bei Umsätzen und Innenumsätzen, die nach dem 31. Dezember 1976 und vor dem 1. Januar 1978 ausgeführt werden, um 50 vom Hundert.

Die Vorschrift des § 4 Abs. 3 Satz 2 und 3 gilt sinngemäß.

(5) Bei geröstetem Kaffee (§ 4 Abs. 1 Nr. 13 Buchstabe a) ist das Entgelt oder Verrechnungsentgelt für die Kürzungen nach § 1 Abs. 1, § 1 a Abs. 1 und § 2 Abs. 1 bei Umsätzen und Innenumsätzen, die nach dem 31. Dezember 1975 und vor dem 1. Januar 1978 ausgeführt werden, um 50 vom Hundert zu mindern.

(6) Die Vorschriften des § 13 a und des § 15 sind erstmals für den Veranlagungszeitraum 1976 anzuwenden.

(7) Die Vorschrift des § 14 Abs. 1 Satz 1 ist erstmals für das Wirtschaftsjahr anzuwenden, das nach dem 31. Dezember 1974 endet.

(8) Die Vorschrift des § 14 Abs. 2 Satz 1 Nr. 2 Buchstabe a Doppelbuchstabe aa ist erstmals auf Gebäude anzuwenden, die nach dem 31. Dezember 1975 hergestellt werden.

(9) Die Vorschriften des § 14 Abs. 2 Satz 2 erster Halbsatz und des § 19 Abs. 2 Satz 1 und Abs. 6 Satz 2 und Satz 4 Nr. 2 sind hinsichtlich des Zeitraums von acht Jahren erstmals auf Schiffe anzuwenden, die nach dem 15. Mai 1973 angeschafft oder hergestellt worden sind. Das gilt nicht für Schiffe, die vom Steuerpflichtigen, bei Gesellschaften im Sinne des § 15 Abs. 1 Ziff. 2 des Einkommensteuergesetzes von der Gesellschaft, nachweislich vor dem 16. Mai 1973 bestellt worden sind oder mit deren Herstellung der Steuerpflichtige vor dem 16. Mai 1973 begonnen hat.

(10) Die Vorschrift des § 14 a Abs. 4 ist erstmals auf Einfamilienhäuser, Zweifamilienhäuser und Eigentumswohnungen anzuwenden, die nach dem 30. November 1974 vom Zweiterwerber angeschafft werden.

(11) Die Vorschrift des § 16 ist hinsichtlich der Worte „Niederlassung Berlin der Industriekreditbank Aktiengesellschaft — Deutsche Industriebank" vom 6. August 1974 an anzuwenden.

(12) Die Vorschrift des § 19 Abs. 1 Satz 4 Nr. 1 ist erstmals auf abnutzbare bewegliche Wirtschaftsgüter anzuwenden, die nach dem 31. Dezember 1975 angeschafft oder hergestellt werden.

(13) Die Vorschriften über die Gewährung der Zulage bei der Zahlung von Konkursausfallgeld sind erstmals ab 20. Juli 1974 anzuwenden.

§ 32

Ermächtigung

Der Bundesminister der Finanzen wird ermächtigt, den Wortlaut dieses Gesetzes in der jeweils geltenden Fassung mit neuem Datum, unter neuer Überschrift und in neuer Paragraphenfolge bekanntzumachen und dabei Unstimmigkeiten des Wortlauts zu beseitigen.

Abschnitt IV

Berlin-Klausel

§ 33

Dieses Gesetz gilt nach Maßgabe des § 12 Abs. 1 und des § 13 Abs. 1 des Dritten Überleitungsgesetzes vom 4. Januar 1952 (Bundesgesetzbl. I S. 1)[11] auch im Land Berlin. Rechtsverordnungen, die auf Grund dieses Gesetzes erlassen werden, gelten im Land Berlin nach § 14 des Dritten Überleitungsgesetzes.

[11] GVBl. S. 394

INDEX

- the numbers refer to the pages -

Kolibri 360 GmbH
Ferdinand-Jühlke-Straße 7
99095 Erfurt, Deutschland
produktsicherheit@kolibri360.de